ABRAHAM FLEXNER: A Flawed American Icon

MICHAEL NEVINS

iUniverse, Inc.
New York   Bloomington

Abraham Flexner: A Flawed American Icon

iUniverse books may be ordered through booksellers or by contacting:

iUniverse
1663 Liberty Drive
Bloomington, IN 47403
www.iuniverse.com
1-800-Authors (1-800-288-4677)

Because of the dynamic nature of the Internet, any Web addresses or links contained in this book may have changed since publication and may no longer be valid. The views expressed in this work are solely those of the author and do not necessarily reflect the views of the publisher, and the publisher hereby disclaims any responsibility for them.

ISBN: 978-1-4502-6086-2 (sc)
ISBN: 978-1-4502-6085-5 (ebook)

Printed in the United States of America

iUniverse rev. date: 10/08/2010

Contents

PREFACE

1940 was a transitional time on both sides of the Atlantic. Europe already was at war; the United States soon would be. Two stimulating books were published that year. *I Remember* was written in anger by Abraham Flexner (1866-1959), an aging educator who had recently been fired from a powerful leadership position - for the second time in a decade. Clearly his purpose was to justify himself, but Flexner had selective memory and the book's opacity perfectly reflected the author's personality.[1]

That same year young John F. Kennedy, a student at Harvard who had spent part of the previous term living with his father in London, wrote his senior thesis *Why England Slept*.[2] The title was an allusion to Winston Churchill's book *While England Slept* which had been written two years earlier. The focus of both Kennedy's and Churchill's books was the mistakes the British government made which had led to war. Ambassador Joseph P. Kennedy, Sr., eager to enhance his son's reputation, had the thesis published and it sold more than 80,000 copies. The author collected $40,000, donated the profits from British sales to victims of Luftwaffe bombings and with the rest bought a green Buick convertible – once again, perfectly reflecting the author's personality.

JFK began his Harvard thesis by quoting British historian B.H.Liddell Hart (1895-1970) whose words accurately described my own purpose in writing this book:

I do not criticize persons,
But only a state of affairs,
It is they, however, who will have to answer for
deficiencies at the bar of history (1933)

Liddell Hart's name is hardly known today, but in his day he was influential and controversial. In 1944 he published a short book with the provocative title *Why Don't We Learn From History?*[3] It contained numerous epigrams and because some of these seemed germane to this project, they are reproduced here in order to frame my analysis of the American icon Abraham Flexner:

What is truth? Many of our troubles arise from the habit, on all sides, of suppressing or distorting what we know quite well is the truth, out of devotion to a cause, an ambition, or an institution – at bottom, this devotion being inspired by our own interest.

Nothing has aided the persistence of falsehood, and the evils resulting from it, more than the unwillingness of good people to admit the truth when it was disturbing to their comfortable assurance.

History has limitations as guiding signpost....for although it can show us the right direction, it does not give detailed information about the road conditions.

When writing the preface to his father's book, Adrian Hart remarked that writing history is a frustrating pursuit: "Just as you think you have unraveled a knotty string of evidence, it coils up in a fresh tangle. Moreover, you can so easily get caught up or tripped up on some awkward and immovable fact just as you seem to be reaching an irresistible conclusion."

That also was my experience, for in the process of thinking about Abraham Flexner I often found myself vacillating between admiration of his notable contributions as an educator and dismay at some of his personal idiosyncrasies. Indeed it was my own ambivalence about him which drove this attempt to capture the essence of the man.

Adrian Hart recalled as well how his father believed that human beings in possession of the facts could by rational process discover the truth about life. However, this discovery was without value unless it was expressed in action as well as education. He valued the moral courage to pursue and propagate truths which might be unpopular or detrimental to one's own or other people's immediate interests. It was necessary to combat misrepresentation or injustice, never to be indifferent or neutral, always to be involved.

Such a viewpoint also might have described Abraham Flexner's attitude, but not entirely. While he could be outspoken and fearless when commenting about issues which pertained directly to education, at times he dissembled, distorted or chose to turn his head. In this respect, Flexner could be an exasperating man.

ENIGMA

Anyone with even scant knowledge of medical history at least has heard of "The Flexner Report" which when published in 1910 helped to transform American medical education from primitive to world class. But nowadays, very few people actually have read the Report and fewer still know anything about the iconic figure who composed it. Yet, when he died in 1959 at age 92 he was lauded in a front-page obituary in the *New York Times*: "No other American of his time contributed more to the welfare of his country and of humanity in general."[1] That's a remarkable eulogy, albeit many of Abraham Flexner's contemporaries would have disagreed.

After completing his Report, Abraham Flexner spent much of the next fifteen years channeling more than half a billion dollars from the Rockefeller Foundation and other philanthropies to favored institutions and in the process, profoundly altered the medical educational landscape. Then in 1930 Flexner reinvented himself as founding director of the Institute for Advanced Study at Princeton where he remained for nearly a decade. Biographic evidence is ample, presumably the most authentic being Flexner's own memoirs – not one, but two of them.

I Remember, published in 1940 shortly after his death, traced a progression from one career triumph to another with the author modestly downplayed his own importance, choosing to present himself as a facilitator rather than an innovator, merely "a humble servant" of power. The book contained numerous engaging anecdotes, but anything which might cast the author in an unfavorable light was omitted. Two decades later and by then in his nineties, Abraham Flexner had a rare second chance to reflect upon his life and times when his publisher persuaded him to compose an updated version of the autobiography. The sequel contained several new chapters about the years after 1940, but despite the passage of time and opportunity to reflect, it provided no new insight.

Thomas Neville Bonner ended his authoritative biography *Iconoclast* of Flexner's "spectacularly powerful career" with this assessment:

> He was fundamentally a deeply gifted human being, warm-hearted, decent and dedicated to his causes and extended family. He was the last American whose interests and activities embraced the entire range of learning, from kindergarten to postgraduate study. He was an innovator possessed of unusual imagination and thick-skinned when it came to criticism. [2]

Bonner described Flexner as combative and fearless in criticizing even the most powerful, adding that "seldom has history produced a figure who so thoughtfully enjoyed controversy and intellectual jousting with those around him." Columbia University historian Allan Nevins [no relation] recalled his good friend as a man of unfailing kindness, lovable, generous, witty, committed to "self-sacrificing effort...for human betterment."[3]

Such reverential accounts notwithstanding, over time as historians have culled archival material a dichotomy has emerged between the public and private Flexner which suggested a more complex portrait than the conventional narrative. Depending on the circumstances, he could be amiable or abrasive, sociable or remote. Daniel M. Fox has suggested that Flexner's heroic self-image was at variance with the facts of his life:

Abraham Flexner was a hero only by identification. His verbal aggressiveness, so dismaying to his colleagues, may have expressed resistance to the routine and forced anonymity of his role as an intellectual servant of other men's power. Flexner was more complicated than his self-image. He could be charming, even obsequious, as well as impatient, aggressively outspoken, and bitterly critical of his colleagues.[4]

John W. Gardner, then President of the Carnegie Corporation, recalled:

In matters of intellect he was forceful, astringent, scornful of compromise, a warrior in behalf of wisdom and virtue, as he conceived them. He had a sparkling wit which was equally effective in mischievous teasing of friends, the needling of those he wished to stir to action, and the harpooning of those who won his scorn... He fought a holy war against slackness, triviality, and educational quackery.[5]

But perhaps it was his equally renowned older brother Dr. Simon Flexner who best captured the personality of the man. Himself intensely introspective, Simon characterized Abe as being completely incapable of a detached point of view about himself, as if self-analysis might weaken his self-assurance:

[He is] a strong person, very generous, intensely egotistical, with a great capacity for self-deception. My belief is that he readily translates events into harmony with his own point of view and his own cogitations. He hardly ever admits mistakes or failure on his own part, although finding many faults in others.[6]

After reviewing his father's unpublished correspondence, Simon's son James Thomas Flexner observed that his uncle's salient characteristics were:

Determination and an ability to lead; a disdain for moving cautiously; glee (which comes out boastfully in the letters) at carrying off complicated and sometimes secret manipulations; a gift for accommodation to sooth the impact of his drives; and boundless energy, which enabled him to remain optimistic in almost any situation.[7]

J.T. Flexner remarked as well about how his father "was annoyed by the sugary descriptions" that were presented in Uncle Abe's autobiography, "so different from his own memories" of their boyhood.[8] To Simon's mind, details of the family's financial circumstances had been exaggerated so as to make their subsequent rise seem more a Horatio Alger story than actually was the fact. Abraham Flexner's justification for writing the updated version of his memoir was typically sanctimonious:

I offer [this book] as an example of what has been done in America by others as well as myself, of what can be done, and of what I believe will always be possible as long as we cling to the ideals of self-reliance, ambition, toleration, and loyalty to what seems to us as individuals worth while, whether or not it seems equally worth while to others.[9]

From diverse descriptions such as these, Abraham Flexner emerges as an enigmatic figure. If sometimes his written words were untrustworthy, equally frustrating were the things that he left unsaid. For example, his memoirs provided no words of explanation about the causes of his two early "retirements," first in 1928 from Rockefeller's General Education Board (GEB) and then a decade later from the Institute for Advanced Study (IAS.) Contrary to official press releases, both departures had been bitter and came about largely as a result of Flexner's prickly personality.

I was especially troubled by how in his writing Flexner was uncharacteristically silent about certain significant social and political matters which were prevalent in this country during the fateful decades between 1910 and 1950 when he was in his prime. Of course, Flexner's focus was on education and it is an author's prerogative to be selective in choosing what to write about. A *New York Times* book reviewer of *I Remember* accurately noted, "The reader must go between the lines to find the personality that the author does not choose to reveal." The reviewer perceived that personality as being "warm, humanitarian, optimistic, loving that 'excellence' which is the key to a surpassingly useful career."[10] Shortly before his death, when Flexner had his second chance to recapitulate, and seemingly still retained full mental faculty, he rather superficially glossed over events of the ensuing years.

Nowadays, when evidence mainly has to be pieced together indirectly from what others said about him, we can only speculate about the reasons for Abraham Flexner's silences. This caveat notwithstanding, Flexner's reticence is troubling because he seems to have known everyone of importance and had a front row seat to such momentous events as two World Wars, Nazism and the Bomb. Nor did the memoirs contain anything about the horrific outcomes of German research which he'd indirectly enabled during the 1920s while working at the Rockefeller Foundation, or even about the Holocaust itself.

Flexner, an assimilated Jew had no use for religion, but never denied his heritage. He believed that it was politically incorrect to call attention to anti-Semitism arguing that to do so would be counterproductive; instead, he claimed that he preferred to work behind the scenes. Perhaps so, but this man who prided himself about always saying what was on his mind, sometimes seemed timid about publicly airing his true beliefs, as if to do so might compromise his influence in the gentile power circles in which he worked and lived. Bonner suggests that Flexner was typical of many secular Jews of his era who "by shedding the habits and religious practices of their parents, by embracing the public schools, by becoming as much like their Protestant countrymen as possible…set out on the road to respectability and fame."[11] In this respect Abraham Flexner certainly was successful.

By design, the title for my work is an oxymoron – how can an icon be flawed? There is an inherent contradiction, as appeared to have been true of the protagonist himself. Surely a plausible case can be made that Flexner's professional career was iconic and various authorities have declared him to have been the most prominent medical educator that America ever has produced. I have no quarrel with such a judgment, nor is it my intent to denigrate Flexner's character his sometime erratic behavior notwithstanding. Indeed I hope to present Abraham Flexner sympathetically – if not necessarily as an icon, then perhaps as a metaphor for a turbulent era when many well-meaning Americans like him refrained from forthrightly addressing prevailing moral issues. Many of them were earnest idealists who trusted that rationality, education and civility would prevail over ignorance, intolerance and barbarism – as it turned out, the Nazis proved them to be deluded.

Writing from the safe perspective of history, it's easy to criticize an earlier generation for its myopia. But while being wary of succumbing to this temptation, neither should we entirely give our predecessors a free pass. Not everyone was passive; indeed many were prescient about the moral hazards facing them. And if we should not be too harsh in judging those who lived in a very different world, it's worthwhile to consider their lives in context, thereby hopefully, to learn from them.

The purpose of this book, then, is to try to separate Abraham Flexner the man from the famous Report which is associated with his name. In so doing I will pay particular attention to Flexner's attitude about two controversial areas, eugenics and anti-Semitism, which although peripheral to his primary focus, may help to provide a useful window both into his personality and into his times.

LOUISVILLE

When Abraham's father Moritz Flexner emigrated from Bohemia in 1853, he followed a familiar narrative: a ninety day passage in steerage followed by an unsuccessful attempt at making a living in New York City.[1,2] Departing from script, Moritz sensed he could make a better living elsewhere and sailed to New Orleans where he contracted a severe case of yellow fever. Once recovered he moved again to join an enclave of Jewish immigrants in Louisville, Kentucky who had fled central Europe after failed mid-century liberal revolts. Moritz Flexner began over as an itinerant peddler with pack on back, then bought a lame horse for four dollars, earned enough to buy a dry goods business and barely survived financial losses during the Civil War and the Panic of 1873. In Louisville he met and married Esther Abraham and the couple had nine children. Abraham (1866-1959) who was sixth in line recalled in his memoir how his parents would say, "Our children will justify us." Indeed, five of the precocious brood and their children would go on to be listed in *Who's Who in America*.

Both parents had limited educations but shared great respect for culture and encouraged their children to read literary classics. Abe was sixteen when his father died, probably of alcoholic liver disease, leaving the family in dire financial straits. At age fifteen young Abraham began earning his way as assistant in the Louisville library. The public schools, a boy's debating society and the library fed his precocious mind. The oldest son Jacob, intelligent and voluble, but thwarted in pursuing his dream of becoming a doctor, turned instead to pharmacy. His drug store soon brought in enough money to pay for two years tuition for his younger brother at Johns Hopkins; seventy five years later Abe would describe his arrival in Baltimore as "the decisive moment of my life." Flexner idolized his mentor President Daniel Coit Gilman whose educational philosophy was modeled after the German university system: Hopkins was a place where "research was the air we breathed."

At age nineteen Abe returned to Louisville where he taught Greek at a public high school, lived at home and gave his entire salary to his mother. In 1890 a wealthy lawyer who was eager to have his unruly son prepare for college arranged with four friends, who also had underachieving sons, to engage Abe as their tutor, paying $500 each. He opened a small private school which soon became known as "Mr. Flexner's School" and provided a proving ground for testing some of Gilman's progressive ideas about education. The school favored small classes, personalized teaching and operated without rules, tests, records or reports. Students could attend classes or not; it was their choice. As described in *I Remember*, Flexner relied upon his own enthusiasm, good humor, cleverness in outwitting his students as they tried to dodge their responsibilities and encouraging competition among them.

Mr. Flexner's School was surprisingly successful and its students were accepted into elite colleges. By 1904 there were thirty six students and five teachers. President Eliot of Harvard asked how he managed to send him boys who were both younger and more capable than students from other schools? Flexner replied "I treated these boys as individuals, and I let each go at his own pace. I took hold of pupils where they were strong, not where they were weak, and having whetted their appetites by success in one field, usually succeeded in arousing their interest in another."

Abe reluctantly agreed to teach a sixteen year old girl, Anne Laziere Crawford; tutored her for a year, and two years later married her. Enough money came in to pay for older brother Simon, who was a late-bloomer, to attend Hopkins and then get a medical degree. Later, when both Abe and Simon were financially solvent, they supported Jake's delayed medical education. Simon Flexner (1863 -1946) went on to become an eminent research biologist who headed the Rockefeller Institute from 1902 to 1935. The brother's careers overlapped and they often were confused for each other. Those who knew Simon at Rockefeller described him as intense, edgy, cold; no one ever called him charming. He was impelled by the desire to promote the institute at all costs and at his memorial service a Nobelist recalled, "Individuals were as nothing to Dr. Flexner compared with the welfare of the institute."[3]

Mr. Flexner's School began to attract pupils from afar and was so successful that his wife complained, "If we don't watch out we shall become rich. Then where would we be?" But after fifteen years Abe became frustrated preparing rich Louisville boys for college. No doubt a little jealous at his brother's success in New York, he complained in a letter to Simon, "I am pathetically anxious to do something, and could were I in reach of publishers and periodicals. But I am fastened here like Prometheus on his rock with a grinding routine that is almost as hard on the liver as a vulture's beak."[4]

When his playwright wife had a theatrical success on Broadway in 1905, Abe decided to close the school in order to resume his own education - first a year at Harvard to get his M.A. and then two years at universities in Berlin and Heidelberg. Having exhausted his funds, he returned to America with a new focus on higher education but no job in sight. His first book, *The American College: A Criticism* (1908) was a scathing critique of the prevailing lecture style which enabled colleges to "handle cheaply by wholesale a large body of students that would otherwise be unmanageable."[5] In it Flexner suggested that the rigid curricula then generally being employed stifled creativity and made no sense. Students should not be distracted by athletics or other extra-curricular activities: "The task of universities is to give society not what it wants, but what it needs….Intellectual inquiry, not job training [is] the purpose of the university."

As for himself a career in teaching was not in the cards. In *I Remember*: he recalled "somehow I came to feel that I was not meant to be a college professor…with all my reverence for learning – and this can hardly be exaggerated – I came to know that my interests were too broad to satisfy with what is now called "a field of concentration."[6]

THE REPORT

Henry S. Pritchett, the president of the new Carnegie Foundation for the Advancement of Teaching, took notice of Flexner's book and was impressed. In 1908 the American Medical Association's Council on Medical Education commissioned the Foundation to perform a detailed study of American medical schools. A pilot study had revealed uniformly low educational standards, especially in the large number of proprietary schools, and the Foundation was selected as a neutral party. President Pritchett's own agenda was to upgrade and recast professional life in America based on the authority of knowledge and skill.

When Pritchett invited the obscure young reformer to head the study, Abraham Flexner's first reaction was that they must have confused him with his brother the doctor. But Pritchett wanted an unbiased lay educator with "an unfettered mind" to take a hard look at the facts and then suggest a plan for reformulating medical education along more scientific lines. Professional schools should be studied not from the point of view of the practitioner but from the standpoint of the educator.

Some Carnegie Foundation board members questioned Pritchett's choice of this unknown layman. Moreover, there were rumors that the young man was hard to get along with. Asked to provide a character reference, Harvard's Dr. William Councilman reported:

I have not known Mr. A. Flexner well, but I have liked what I have seen of him. I should think he might be somewhat erratic and probably hasty to judgment, but a very able and valuable man for all that. I think it more or less easy to explain why he should not be a *persona grata* to many of the men at Harvard just at present, for his book criticized many of the conditions at the college, and I have never found that men take very kindly to criticism especially when it comes from the outside.[1]

The Carnegie Foundation appointed Flexner to their research staff and between January 1909 and April 1910, he personally visited all 155 schools throughout the United States and Canada, usually accompanied by a member of the AMA's Council on Education. Sometimes he revisited institutions so the total number of site visits actually was 175, most done within an eight month period. Never previously having set foot within a medical school, he was determined to learn everything about them by "going about....swiftly." He used no standard questionnaire and sometimes investigations were made unannounced. Generally he was well received, perhaps because as Carnegie's emissary his hosts felt that making a good impression might lead to subsidies.

When Flexner's findings were published in June 1910, they caused a sensation; fifteen thousand copies were distributed free and summaries provided to popular magazines. Henry Pritchett wrote the Report's Introduction and his blunt comments gave a sense of what would follow:

For twenty-five years past there has been an enormous over-production of uneducated and ill trained medical practitioners. This has been in absolute disregard of the public welfare and without any serious thought of the interests of the public.Taking the United States as a whole, physicians are four or five times as numerous in proportion to population as in older countries like Germany. Over-production of ill-trained men is due in the main to the existence of a very large number of commercial schools, sustained in many cases by advertising methods through which a mass of unprepared youth is drawn out of industrial occupations into the study of medicine.[2]

With few exceptions medical schools were private ventures conducted for profit. Applicants who could pay the tuition seldom were turned down for lack of scholarship by unsavory "diploma mills" at a time when their certificates alone were a license to practice. At the turn of the century Johns Hopkins was the only medical school to require an undergraduate degree for entrance and 140 of the schools Flexner visited had no library. He described conditions at one college as "sordid, hideous, unintelligent even when honest – and so little that is even honest."

These were typical assessments: California Medical College, "The school is a disgrace to the State whose laws permit its existence." At Tufts College Medical School, "Entrance requirement below an actual high school." In New York State, "Despite the University charter, the University of Buffalo is a fiction." In Georgia at the College of Eclectic Medicine and Surgery, "Nothing more disgraceful calling itself a Medical School can be found anywhere." A faculty member at North Carolina Medical College was quoted as saying, "It is idle to talk of real laboratory work for students so ignorant and clumsy. Many of them, gotten through advertising, would make better farmers."[3]

Abraham Flexner's 389 page Bulletin No. 4, *Medical Education in the United States and Canada: A Report to the Carnegie Foundation for the Advancement of Teaching* although never officially endorsed by the AMA was fully supported by them. It recommended that medical schools need to be properly equipped and linked to first-rate hospitals, students must be well qualified and research should be "untrammeled by near reference to practical ends."

The Report's author's name has sometimes been used as an adjective "flexnerian," to signify strong support of basic science in medical school curricula. Abraham Flexner had a passion for order and efficiency and in subsequent works provided a clear road map for the future. What he envisioned was a close bond between the basic sciences, organized professional medicine and university education; faculty and administration united by their mutual goal of excellence in all things. Medical science should be taught in university settings so that graduates could better understand the world in which they and their patients lived – physicians should be broadly educated, not merely technicians; they needed to have "insight and empathy."

There should be fewer but better physicians and the vast majority of schools eliminated or consolidated into stronger units. In fact, support for many of Flexner's ideas had been growing for years, but the Report's effect was sufficient that schools either would have to raise their standards or fail. The existence of many schools was precarious anyway and most quack schools already were teetering on the brink of bankruptcy -- the Report provided a timely nudge. Although Flexner's goal for no more than thirty-one schools was never realized; by 1922 only eighty-one schools survived, (today, there are 127) most being closely linked to universities.[4]

Flexner's comments inevitably created both friends and enemies and the Report was described variously as being "unfair," "flippant," "full of errors," "impudent." When criticized that many of his site visits had been cursory, Flexner responded, "You don't need to eat a whole sheep to know it's tainted."[5] One physician regretted that Flexner had not been kicked down the front steps – that failure to do so was "a reflection on medical manhood." There was one death threat. The *Medical Record*, a weekly journal, editorialized:

> What the writer [Flexner] does not seem to have discovered is that all these schools, with the exception of a very small and practically negligible number, are in the process of betterment....When one realizes what

the best of medical schools were twenty-five or thirty years ago, and what tremendous progress has been made during the past twenty, and especially, the past ten years, and when one remembers that all this uplift has come from within, without the help of any outside "Foundation" the work of Mr. Flexner seems somewhat a waste of effort and a needless expenditure of Mr. Carnegie's hard earned money.[6]

Latter day historians sometimes have argued that Flexner's personal influence was not as great as touted. Lester King, for one, began his critique, "The so-called Flexner report… is probably the most grossly overrated document in American medical history.…endowed with canonical status that has resulted in some horrendous distortion of the historical record."[7]

Some critics scolded him as a dogmatic elitist who spent other people's money on his own pet projects. The closing or mergers of inferior schools eliminated many that provided training for women and minorities but historian Howard Merkel has cautioned against the inclination to view history through today's prism: "The real issue is that the good old days were not that good anyway, and to put it all on his lap is too much. American society was harsh and closed to women and blacks and remained that way for decades."[8]

Others chided the Report's author for not seeming to understand that there was an art of medicine as well as a science: "His [Flexner's] language leaves little doubt that he held the mass produced "family doctor" in low esteem and considered the *ne plus ultra* among physicians to be the highly scientific and sophisticated clinician moulded in the Hopkins environment or its equivalent."[9]

Harvard's Francis Peabody complained that Flexner's approach weakened "the soul of the clinic" and pleaded for a more patient-oriented, less academic place to reach medical students and for "more of the spirit that gives life."[10]

The eminent William Osler, now ensconced at Oxford but still loyal to his former colleagues at Johns Hopkins, criticized Flexner's call for full-time clinical faculty which he described as the "climax of doctrinary madness." Although Bulletin No. 4 had contained nothing about full time faculty, this idea was integral to Flexner's hidden agenda which soon leaked out and emerged as the most contentious area of discord. Osler excused Flexner's "perhaps pardonable ignorance of a layman," but feared that his approach would begin "the evolution of a set of clinical prigs, the boundary of whose horizon would be the laboratory." Concerning the implication that clinicians were profiting from the current system:

> Do not be led away by the opinions of the pure laboratory men, who have no knowledge of the clinical situation and its needs...Against the sin of prosperity, which looms large in Mr. Flexner's Report, the clinical professor must battle hard. I was myself believed to be addicted to it...but I took out of Baltimore not one cent of all the fees...I received in the sixteen years of my work.[11]

A measure of the enduring legacy of the Flexner Report is the fact that every twenty-five years or so since 1910, symposia and published reviews have appeared in order to assess progress in medical education and to list problems which still need to be addressed. On the occasion of the Report's centennial in 2010, an issue of *Academic Medicine* was devoted to evaluating Flexner's legacy. In one commentary, Professor Kenneth Ludmerer noted that for nearly a century Flexner has been both credited and blamed for things he did not do and suggests that some of his greatest contributions were unappreciated. Among these he had transformed medical education into a broad social movement, aligning it with John Dewey's philosophy of "progressive" education and what worked at the elementary school level, learning by doing, was applicable at all educational levels.[12]

Dr. Ludmerer attempted to dispel various myths associated with the Report including "the fiction that little had transpired in medical education until Flexner "in one stunning blow, modernized an anachronistic system." He described Flexner as being more flexible than commonly supposed; rather, in his university-based, research-oriented conception of medical education no idea was too sacrosanct to reform or review. Flexner had written, "This solution deals only with the present and the near future, - a generation at most. In the course of the next thirty years needs will develop of which we here take no account. As we cannot foretell them, we shall not endeavor to meet them."

According to Ludmerer, Flexner's gift to medical education and the medical profession was, and continues to be, an unswerving commitment to excellence and public service.[13] Bulletin No. 4 was followed about two years later by Bulletin No. 6, also commissioned by the Carnegie Foundation, which was based on a whirlwind survey of medical education in England, France and Germany. As he later described,

> I had worked at it as I had worked at the other, with unremitting zeal and at a pace that now seems to me as I look back, half mad. But these were glorious days. I was young, enthusiastic, and strong, and every day brought me into contact with men of superior wisdom, culture, and experience. Writing up my notes kept me at work till the small hours of the morning, for there were no secretaries in those days to whom one could dictate between teatime and dinner the results of a hard day spent in observation and discussion.[14]

THE BOARD

The Federal government didn't support basic science research and medical education until after World War II so funding was substantially dependent upon the generosity of wealthy individuals who donated through family foundations. Although it was officially denied, including by Flexner, the personal interests of the moguls often influenced how their money would be spent. Whether their motives were shrewd business instincts or *noblesse oblige*, the influence of these industrialists and financiers was profound, some would say pernicious.

Never well known to the public, John D. Rockefeller, Jr. has been described both as "a blessing to mankind" or as a bane. His grandfather "Big Bill" had been a traveling "snake oil" salesman and his father relied on a homeopathic physician for his own care, but during the first half of the 20th century, the Rockefeller name would become identified with the transformation of medical education and research. The General Education Board (GEB) when founded in 1902 was dedicated to promoting education within the United States "without distinction of race, sex or creed." It was the Rockefeller's first venture into philanthropy but the real moving force was a dynamic Baptist minister, Frederick Gates.

JDR, Jr. was not particularly interested in the intricacies of medical educational organization as much as he wished to use his foundations to study the causes of societal discord and to mold Americans to his concept of "perfect human nature." As he saw it, society was becoming chaotic and proactive measures were needed in order to preserve the American way of life. Poverty, alcoholism, mental illness and licentiousness all could be corrected by policies which restricted immigration, banned intermarriage and segregated or sterilized the biologically defective.

Rockefeller's ambitious goal was to promote the well-being of mankind throughout the world. Toward that end, he was interested in finding practical ways to regulate these scourges. Obsessed with maintaining social order, he accepted hereditarian science as a way of benefiting mankind but some Foundation leaders had more radical ideas: John Foster Dulles, for one, declared that by eliminating the weakest members of the population a purer race could be created.

Rockefeller, Jr. was so impressed with Flexner's report on medical education that he engaged the young reformer to study the nature of modern prostitution in Europe in the hope that the findings could be adapted in the United States. Applying himself to the task with his usual thoroughness, for two years Flexner interviewed police officials, women in and out of brothels and social workers. When *Prostitution in Europe* was published by the Bureau of Social Hygiene, Junior himself wrote a glowing introduction. In it Flexner suggested that the best remedy for eliminating prostitution was to prevent it from originating in the first place and, as with other social problems, a rational program of education and science was required.[1] Historian Nicholas R. Scott has noted that "Flexner's conclusions are extremely important because of their relevance with eugenics theory and their profound effect on Rockefeller, Jr. Indeed the book's description of the causes of prostitution were the very same elements that eugenicists claimed to have found among the feebleminded."[2] More about this shortly.

Having completed the prostitution study to Rockefeller's satisfaction, in October, 1913 Flexner was offered the position of assistant secretary of the Foundation's General Education Board (GEB.) working directly under Wallace Buttrick for a munificent salary of seventy-five hundred dollars. Andrew

Carnegie and Henry Pritchett realized they couldn't match the amounts that Rockefeller and Gates were prepared to devote, fully eight times more, and gave Flexner their blessing. However, Carnegie was skeptical and doubted that medical establishment leaders could be changed. Flexner rebutted, "I don't propose to change them. I propose to get rid of them." Carnegie: "I'll get you back." Flexner: "No you won't." In a letter to brother Simon, Abe exulted, "And so opens a new chapter."

Abraham Flexner quickly gained influence on the GEB. By the end of the first year he was elected to the policymaking board of trustees and three years later was named its secretary. In this capacity he mastered the art of administrative politics and was a central figure in the emerging phenomenon of corporate philanthropy; his views had equal weight with other board members and he defended his positions vigorously. Although the GEB's role supposedly was limited to improving medical education in America, in the early years delegation of policy making was informal, the various Rockefeller philanthropies were a veritable mosaic of overlapping groups, and Flexner was given relatively free rein. By the early 1920s all inquiries about medical education were directed to him and Board members would consistently defer to his judgment on a broad range of issues.

In his memoirs Flexner recalled how once while lunching with Buttrick and Gates, he'd remarked, "I have often wondered why I was asked to come into the General Education Board." Gates replied, "Because Buttrick and I decided that you would think of things that would not occur to us...I had thus received a sort of roving commission."[3] The roving ambassador felt free to network with colleagues in Britain and western Europe, but in time this loose arrangement created confusion which led to reorganization and diminution of his influence.

In Flexner's first years at the GEB, he suggested that if Mr. Rockefeller would lead the way by giving fifty million dollars, much more could be added from other sources in the form of matching grants. Recommendations from Bulletin No. 4 were implemented under his persuasive guidance such that between

1902 and 1934, donations of more than $600 million were made for medical education – about $90 million coming from the Rockefeller Foundation, $154 million from other philanthropic foundations and an additional $450 million from non-foundation sources.

Flexner was adept at extracting large gifts from wealthy entrepreneurs, including the likes of Andrew Carnegie, J.P.Morgan, Julius Rosenwald, Payne Whitney and Albert Lasker. Always a shrewd negotiator, Flexner had the coolness of a gambler knowing just when to play his cards in order to coax larger contributions than the donors had intended. In a letter to a friend George Eastman described him as "the worst highwayman that ever flitted into and out of Rochester."

> He put up a job on me and cleaned me out of a thundering lot of my hard-earned savings. I have just heard that he is coming up here in June to speak at the graduating exercises of the "allied" hospitals. I have been asked to sit on the stage with him, but instead of that I shall probably flee from town for fear he will hypnotize me again.[4]

Flexner was capable of compromising if necessary in order to achieve the best possible result, but when things didn't go his way his charms could wear thin and sometimes his dogmatism created bitter enemies. Considering his lack of scholarly background, it's easy to understand how university presidents and members of the medical establishment might take offense at his self-assurance.

In 1925 Flexner praised progress in American medical education which had occurred during fifteen years since the Report, but noted there still were great gaps, especially that clinical teaching relied too much on busy practitioners and students often were poorly prepared in humanistic studies. In an exchange of letters with Harvard's Dr. Harvey Cushing he characterized the majority of currently practicing physicians as "chauffeurs," capable of following orders but not of keeping up with the advances of a rapidly growing profession.[5]

Flexner advised that more attention should be paid to the geographic distribution of practitioners and in a confidential memorandum named those schools which ought to survive and would receive financial assistance – notably Vanderbilt, Iowa, Washington of St. Louis, Rochester, Rush in Chicago, Cornell, Columbia, Yale and his favorite, Johns Hopkins.[6] He felt that negroes needed there own physicians because they were a "potential source of infection and contagion" and had recommended that the seven existing negro medical schools be reduced to two: Meharry and Howard – "the negro needs good schools rather than many schools."[7] Between 1902 and 1929 Rockefeller appropriations to support negro education amounted to more than $20 million.

Most of the favored schools were in financial trouble and were willing to yield to Flexner's terms; contracts between the GEB and participating schools required that the money would have to be returned if they deviated from the agreed upon plan. Sociologist Paul Starr has suggested that the grants determined "not so much which institutions would survive as which would dominate, how they would be run, and what ideals would prevail."[8] A standard curriculum was proposed for all schools, not just for a few research-oriented centers, and frequently there were bitter struggles for control between old-line practitioners and the insurgent research scientists.

Because foundations had been coming under increasing criticism from the public and the government for manipulative practices, GEB leaders insisted that they were merely a conduit to provide the necessary means requested by the universities and that the gifts had no strings attached. Wishing to avoid controversy, what the Rockefeller managers said publicly often was not reflected in their private correspondence. In fact, the GEB didn't issue public reports during its first twelve years until Flexner began doing so anonymously in 1914.

In later years Abraham Flexner grudgingly agreed that greater flexibility was called for, akin to graduate education in the arts and sciences. Even at the few truly excellent schools, uniform curricula placed too little responsibility on students who Flexner claimed would become like "schoolchildren" if standards were imposed through bureaucratic administration by persons of inferior scientific and professional training.

Flexner sometimes wrote about the virtues of "democracy" in the abstract, but in practice what he meant was considerably less than broad consensus -- egalitarian processes would be incompatible with imposition of standards by organizational leaders. As he explained in his autobiography, he and his colleagues at the foundations "never pretended to have an original idea [but] we knew educational strategy [and] worked together informally, without rules or organization. We needed no organization."[9]

What Foundations can accomplish depends upon their having in them men with ideas – definite sound ideas, based on wide and thorough knowledge of our own and other countries in different fields of interest… Foundation officers who are to be constructive contributors to social progress, need then to be forceful, analytical, imaginative and well-informed [like him] if foundations are to be fertile, rather than sterile.[10]

Abraham Flexner was the dominant personality among the Rockefeller officers and few dared to cross him, but as younger men joined the Board there were jealousies and turf wars. One of the young Turks, Alan Gregg admired Flexner's organizational skills but recalled that he was rarely accessible to underlings and was most effective as a back-room negotiator. His management style at Rockefeller, and later in Princeton, was to call a conference which then would form a committee which, in turn, would issue a report. This gambit gave the appearance of broad participation, but Flexner manipulated every step of the process. Among his fellow workers he gained a reputation for hard work, solitude, obstinacy and innovative ideas. While he could display enormous tact when necessary, these traits were matched by "a formidable intransigence."[11]

As his power grew, Flexner sometimes outmaneuvered former mentors like Henry Pritchett and Frederick Gates over policy matters and even criticized old friends like William Welch and Milton Winternitz. To Edward Embree, Secretary of the Rockefeller Foundation, Flexner expressed his disdain for most physicians and medical educators: "In medical education there is but one God…Profit! Amen." He called the AMA the "advertising center in medical education [which] for years tried to make the world think that Chicago was the medical center of this country."[12] Scientific medicine was incompatible with commercialism and clinicians were "too easy victims for the encroachment of profitable practice." Flexner's solution was to "protect" physicians from temptation by prohibiting private practice, making them employees on fixed salaries.

His self-righteousness offended and often alienated colleagues who, from his viewpoint, should have been less timid. As Flexner saw it, "We have in America no way of achieving rational ends by voluntary submission to rational ideals." Firm leadership was required. In his opinion, the same was true at the GEB where after Wallace Buttrick retired no one in authority was particularly interested in his programs which, as a result, dwindled from inattention.

Not only did Flexner's autocratic leadership style create "wounded spirits" within the Board, but as he became marginalized he began drawing increasing criticism from the outside. Bacteriologist Hans Zinsser regretted the growing power of foundations over educational decisions of universities, noting that too many conditions were attached to each grant and that there was danger that control was passing to a "self-perpetuating body of gentlemen." Pointedly, among them was "a capable scholar who has made himself one of the foremost lay students of medical education."[13]

To his dismay, Flexner was passed over in 1923 as President of the GEB. Two years later he resigned as secretary but retained his position as director of the Division of Medical Education.

He took several extended leaves of absence and during his last five years at Rockefeller became increasingly frustrated by bureaucratic struggle. In a letter to Wallace Buttrick he complained,

> We have become too highly organized, have too many projects, too much conscientious attention to machinery, far far too little intellectual loafing and browsing....The offices are in my opinion a less stimulating place for a young man today than they were in the easy-going days when I came in and you and Mr. Gates and Page would sit down and just talk, leaving me to listen, learn and be infinitely stimulated. An efficiency expert who stuck his head in the door in those days would have exclaimed, "What a waste of time!", but I can never be sufficiently grateful for what those rambling, illuminating, leisurely talks meant in opening my eyes and broadening my horizon.[14]

Alan Gregg observed that as his jurisdiction and influence waned, Flexner was "terrifically jealous of his job and any apparent incursions or intrusions."[15] Friends urged him to compromise but that wasn't his way. Rockefeller Foundation reorganization at the end of 1927 transferred many of his powers to some whom he considered unqualified. When leadership of the GEB was offered to Trevor Arnett, he was unwilling to accept if Flexner remained. JDR, Jr: was advised that Arnett "would not consider the Presidency if Abe were left in the picture...the situation would be impossible...something will have to be found for Abe or he will have to be retired."[16]

Rockefeller tactfully tried to ease him out by offering a position on his personal staff which was refused. But by March, 1928, Flexner could hold out no longer. He implied that at age 62, he was approaching the mandatory retirement age of 65 and that he welcomed the opportunity to engage in other activities. His annual salary of $20,000 would be continued until his sixty-fifth birthday; thereafter, it would be set at $10,000 a year for life.

In a letter to colleagues on the Board, addressed as "my friends" he assured that while he retired with "the most cordial and friendly personal relations," his presence under the new conditions might prove an "embarrassment" to those who had the responsibility of conducting the new organization. A public statement issued by the Board (May 25, 1928) accepted Flexner's withdrawal "with great regret," stressed that his retirement was "entirely voluntary," praised him for his many years of successful service and offered "unqualified good wishes."

At the time of this announcement, Flexner was away in England delivering a series of lectures at Oxford and skeptical newspaper reporters had to ask his brothers Bernard and Simon for an explanation. They denied knowing the reason for his choice or that there had been any trouble with the Board. In fact, Abe wrote to Simon that the "sudden guillotining of a life's work," had left him stunned and angry: "my mind has not ceased to marvel at either the folly or the brutality of what has been done."[17]

None of this melodrama was mentioned in *I Remember,* only a vague statement that when he "chose" to retire, he took a temporary position at Oxford. Omitting any nasty details, he hoped he would not be considered "immodest" for including the full text of Rockefeller's letter of regret -- a portion of which follows:

> I think it would be hard to overestimate the contribution which you have made to the development of education generally in the United States and especially to the establishment of a high, strong foundation of medical education. In the fifteen years of your relationship to the General Education Board, because of the splendid background of knowledge which you have brought with you and your highly trained mind, you have been able to

accomplish what another could not have done in twice the time, if at all.[18]

If Flexner's true feelings were publicly unspoken, they were bitterly evident in a letter to his wife which repeated almost exactly what he'd written to Simon.

It is no simple business to sit by and see your life's work strangled or mutilated....My mind has not ceased to marvel at either the folly or the brutality of what has been done to me...I am clear that I am not wanted – indeed only docile and mediocre talents are required.... Let us wait and see what five years hence will be said about the wisdom of those who have participated in this debacle.[19]

Years later, his nephew James T. Flexner had a more objective perspective:

As success and power came to Abraham, the lack of self-confidence that had held him back until he was almost forty was replaced by its opposite. When he could not persuade, he trampled over. To Simon's dismay he scolded even Dr. Welch. Despite his brother's efforts to restrain him in 1928 Abraham forced his alienation and subsequent resignation from the Rockefeller philanthropies.[20]

Once he was safely out of the way, his former critic Hans Zinsser was quoted as saying:

Oh Abraham Flexner! We have fought with you...have alternatively admired and disliked you, have applauded your wisdom and detested you for opinionatedness (sic). But in just retrospect, layman as you are, we hail you as the father – or, better, the uncle of modern medical education in America.[21]

Not one to slink away, Flexner continued to publish and in his next book *Universities, American, English, German* (based on his Rhodes Trust lectures at Oxford in 1928) he was in a provocative mood: "I am having a lot of fun especially with my own country, which is much madder than I expected." Friends urged him to scale back the aggressive tone but he seemed eager to settle scores: "I expect to be skinned alive" by American university presidents. No wonder; he described the Harvard Graduate School of Business as "pretentious" and "dangerous." "Giving full credit for all that was good, I riddled with facts, sarcasm and documents the outright and shameless humbuggery that was proving profitable at teachers' colleges; in home study courses at Columbia, Chicago, and even my own beloved Johns Hopkins." The Columbia University School of Journalism he placed "on a par with university faculties of cookery and clothing."

When a suggestion was made that the League of Nations assume responsibility for international medical education, his close colleague Raymond Fosdick, who supported the idea, asked his opinion. The acerbic reply was vintage AF:

> I have walked in the deep forests of Scarsdale [and] pondered the weighty educational problems upon which you consult the oracle...For the present, I should not even consider your compromise [an outside international body connected with the League.] I'd stop, look and listen for a while and see whether the thing can make good on its immediate tasks....
>
> Our system of medical education is better than the English or the French because we have learned from both England and Germany and adapted the hints to American conditions....in education one need not be wholly indigenous – and had better not be. But the League of Nations, just being born, isn't a promising agent of international educational suggestion and initiative....

Everything desirable and attainable depends in the last resort on education, but it doesn't follow that the League would be wise to undertake to be *an* or *the* international educational dynamo…Before you fellows act, get to me facts about definite needs and possibilities – don't go off half-cocked. The League had better, for the present stick to jobs it can't escape, instead of going after jobs of questionable appropriateness….It's all the difference between having something to do and having to do something.[22]

Having been "retired," Abraham Flexner was restless and in a pugnacious mood -- but at this point I will interrupt the narrative flow in order to expand upon a phenomenon which already has been mentioned several times. During the first quarter of the 20th century, eugenics theory appealed to many people, sometimes effected government policies and would contribute to horrific events in Europe. As often was the case, Abraham Flexner left no distinct paper trail so we can only infer what his personal beliefs may have been about this important issue.

EUGENICS

The term "eugenics" (well-born) was coined in 1883 by the English scientist Sir Francis Galton. It was substantially derived from the work of his cousin Charles Darwin and often defined as "the science of breeding better humans" - some spoke of breeding a race of human thoroughbreds. At various times and to different degrees eugenics was endorsed by such luminaries as Theodore Roosevelt, Woodrow Wilson, Herbert Hoover, Alexander Graham Bell, Luther Burbank, Havelock Ellis, Winston Churchill, George Bernard Shaw and H.G.Wells. It was an era when many people believed that science, technology, and education could solve society's ills and, to be sure, there was nothing particularly evil about encouraging the best and brightest of society to be fruitful and multiply.[1]

Eugenicists sincerely believed that selective breeding would save the human race from inevitable decline and that behavior was more influenced by heredity than by environment; in effect, that nature trumped nurture. Eugenics theory had so-called "positive" and "negative" aspects with proponents of the latter discouraging propagation of those whom they perceived to be biologic inferiors – including "half-breeds," "morons," epileptics, Eastern and Southern European immigrants and the like. Little if any concern was expressed about human dignity or individual rights.

At the movement's epicenter in Cold Spring Harbor, Long Island, Charles Davenport and Harry Laughlin championed forcibly sterilizing those Americans deemed to be genetically inferior, ten percent at a time. Once "the lower tenth" (roughly fourteen million) was out of the way, the process would be repeated until only the fittest survived – "social Darwinism" run amuck. Financial support for eugenics research and policy development came primarily from the Harriman, Carnegie and Rockefeller Foundations.

Harry Laughlin was an effective fund raiser who liked to flatter his donors: "Vastly more effective than ten million dollars to 'charity' would be ten million to Eugenics. He who, by such a gift, should redeem mankind from vice, imbecility and suffering would be the world's wisest philanthropist."[2] Laughlin once declared, "To purify the breeding stock of the race at all costs is the slogan of eugenics...The mothers of unfit children should be relegated to a place comparable to that of the females of mongrel strains of domestic animals."[3]

Margaret Sanger, the famous birth control crusader, saw eugenics as a way to lower the birth rate of such undesirables as "Hebrews, Slavs, Catholics and Negroes." Her slogan was "More children for the fit; less for the unfit." California agriculturist Paul Popenoe wrote that sterilization is "one of many measures the state can and must use to protect itself from racial deterioration." The idea was to eliminate "bad seeds" and, in time, 20,000 Californians would be surgically altered. Popenoe's book was admired by the new Nazi government and translated into German.

The prominent environmentalist and founder of the Bronx Zoo Madison Grant wrote an influential book *The Passing of the Great Race* (1916) which was so admired by young Adolf Hitler that he wrote a fan letter telling Grant that the book was his own personal Bible. Madison Grant argued that democracy is unable to progress when two races of unequal value live side by side. He believed in the superiority of the blue-eyed, fair–haired Nordic race; Hitler called them "Aryans."

During World War I, a committee headed by Robert Yerkes devised simplistic intelligence tests which when used on nearly two million army recruits "proved" that 47% of whites generally,

70% of Jews and 89% of negroes were unfit for military service. In a 1924 ruling in the case of *Buck v. Bell*, the United States Supreme Court upheld a Virginia law which favored coerced sterilization. Chief Justice Oliver Wendell Holmes, Jr., himself a student of eugenics, ruled that a deficient mother, daughter and granddaughter justified the need for sterilization. He famously concluded: "It is better for all the world, if instead of waiting to execute degenerate offspring for crime or let them starve for their imbecility, society can prevent those who are manifestly unfit from continuing their kind....Three generations of imbeciles are enough."

While it's true that eugenics had great currency early in the last century, many astute observers understood what was at stake and spoke out boldly. As early as 1913, when New Jersey's Supreme Court overturned the state's sterilization law for those deemed unfit to propagate, Chief Justice Charles Garrison wrote, "If the enforced sterility law of this class be a legitimate exercise of government power, a wide field of legislative activity and duty is thrown open to which it would be difficult to assign a legal limit....Racial differences, for instance, might afford a basis for such an opinion in communities where that question is unfortunately a permanent and paramount issue."[4]

Concerning race-based intelligence testing, journalist Walter Lippman minced no words: "There is danger of perversion by muddle-headed and prejudiced men....if misused, intelligence testing could become an engine of cruelty.....[the testing movement was becoming] the happy hunting grounds of quacks and snobs."

Influenced by this pseudoscience, in 1924 Congress enacted immigration quotas against nations of "inferior stock," in effect, closing America's "golden door." A decade later this would cut off an escape route for millions of Europeans. According to historian Stephen Jay Gould, "The eugenicists battled and won one of the greatest victories of scientific racism in American history."[5]

By 1937 eugenics had seeped into the American culture to such an extent that a Gallup poll found 84% of American approved sterilization of the mentally ill. By 1939 some 400,000 Germans had been sterilized before more efficient methods of eliminating the unwanted were devised. The United States, which began the trend earlier in the century, now lagged far behind – one eugenicist complained that the Germans were beating us at our own game. By the 1970s some 65,000 Americans had been forcibly sterilized.

Considering this deplorable story, it's reasonable to ask to what extent, if at all, Abraham Flexner endorsed eugenics ideology? At best, the evidence is mixed and the word "eugenics" does not appear in either of his memoirs. In 1912 the Carnegie Foundation had sent Flexner abroad to study European medical schools and his new report (Bulletin No. 6) had similar impact as Bulletin No. 4. Once again Henry Pritchett wrote a lengthy introduction and had a broader agenda than medical education reform. By then eight states had passed legislation which would permit coercive segregation or sterilization of feebleminded and epileptic people. A review of Flexner's new report published in *The Popular Science Monthly* noted, "The Carnegie Foundation places itself in the position of the practical eugenicist who would put unfit parents out of the way. This is a delicate and difficult undertaking which one is scarcely prepared to entrust to Dr. Pritchett and Mr. Flexner."[6]

Whether or not Abraham Flexner advocated "negative" eugenics policies, he was surrounded by outspoken eugenicist colleagues who did, the likes of Rockefeller, Jr., Alexis Carrel, Charles Lindbergh, Henry Pritchett, Raymond and Harry Fosdick, Alan and John Foster Dulles. As a youth Flexner had been influenced by Herbert Spenser, the philosopher who popularized the theory of "social Darwinism" and coined the expression, "survival of the fittest." But even if he might have been sympathetic to some aspects of eugenics theory, it's likely that any such views would have evolved as the implications of implementing "negative" policies gradually became evident to all.

Speaking in a commencement speech to Jewish social workers in September, 1928 Flexner remarked that there was "nothing on the face of the earth about which more nonsense [has] been uttered than the subject of racial characteristics."[7] He doubted whether there had ever been a Nordic race and stated that it was absurd to apply terms like Protestant, Catholic or Jewish to this nation and urged the graduates to remember that they were "Americans as well as Jews." A reporter praised him for speaking out against the idea of "pure-blooded race" and for knocking out "the Nordic straw man." However, by the time of this speech much of the damage already had been done in this country -- restrictive immigration policies had been enacted and the Supreme Court's decision in *Buck v. Bell* had paved the way for many states to pass coercive sterilization laws.

Flexner's message to the social workers notwithstanding, it was at variance with programs he helped establish during his long association with the Rockefeller Foundation. The German economy was crippled after World War I ended and on an exhausting visit to Germany in July 1922, Flexner found things vastly changed:

> Now two decades later the lakes and the mountains and the skies – they are all the same – but the Europe for which they furnished the background has perished. It is not only that we have grown older, though doubtless that is a factor, but the war has destroyed the tranquility, and for all we know, may have ruined European civilization.... The universities are impoverished and men are looking like shipwrecked sailors in every direction for some hope of aid and comfort....Things are, I believe, in all the warring countries rather worse than I was willing to believe.[8]

Flexner described Berlin as a stricken city and, unbidden, prepared a plan to help medical scientists in German universities. He advised leaders of the Rockefeller Foundation of the urgency of the situation and sent back detailed reports requesting substantial support for scientists who amidst the chaos came to realize that American philanthropists could be their salvation. Fearing that scientific activity was near collapse, but distrusting universities which had nurtured nationalism in the past, the New York office began providing fellowships to gifted young researchers which by 1926 would amount to the equivalent of $4 million through various Rockefeller programs. These funds were funneled through their Paris office to a committee of scientists headed by Professor Heinrich Poll[9]

When he'd visited Germany in 1910, Flexner had established a warm friendship with Poll who had done pioneering work on twins and participated in state-sponsored committees on social engineering. Professor Poll was a founding member of the Kaiser Wilhelm Institute for Anthropology, Human Heredity and Eugenics and an adviser to the Prussian Ministry of Health. As described by historian Edwin Black:

> To literally save German science, Rockefeller money – *guided by Flexner's recommendations* [my italics] -- came to the rescue in November, 1922....The foundation inaugurated its own special funding committee. Flexner selected his longtime Berlin friend Heinrich Poll to lead the committee. Poll had assisted Flexner in his earlier survey of German medical schools. Poll also was a leading eugenicist ...lectured extensively on hereditary traits and feeblemindedness.....Quickly, Rockefeller's freely flowing money, distributed by Poll became a forceful and intrusive factor in German research... leading German researchers were grumbling to each other about 'King Poll' whom they said exercised an intolerable control over Rockefeller grants and therefore German science itself.[10]

Ironically, Heinrich Poll was victimized by the very policies he helped put into place. Born to Jewish parents he'd converted to Protestantism when young, but when the Nazis came to power in 1933 was forced to resign his position at the University of Hamburg. Abraham Flexner arranged for Poll to deliver the first speech in a lecture series his brother Bernard endowed in his name at Vanderbilt University, but despite Poll's connections and even his offer to wash test tubes, he was unable to secure permanent entry to America. In 1939 "King Poll" escaped to safe haven in Sweden, where a few days after arrival he suddenly died of a heart attack. On hearing the news his Christian wife committed suicide.

Elitists on the Rockefeller and Carnegie boards supported studying the mechanisms of evolution as a possible way to preserve the social order and many of their funding decisions were shaped by this belief. Raymond Fosdick, Rockefeller Junior's "closest and most trusted adviser," stressed "few matters are more pressingly important" than this problem which was "a basic cause of social degeneration and disorder." Indeed in 1921 prominent scientists met at the Carnegie Institute in Washington to study the fundamental similarities of "the monkey, the baby and the idiot"[11]

When GEB Secretary Edwin Embree visited Europe in 1926, he contacted German biologists who intended to merge human heredity and eugenics into a single discipline. Flexner did not take exception, but counseled discretion: "The Rockefeller Foundation should not itself undertake studies particularly in such controversial topics as population and eugenics. The fact that [the Foundation] is not proposing to enter directly into such fields should be made clear from the outset." This implied that *indirect* sponsorship might be permissible through intermediaries, which is exactly what had been happening for the past four years.

Rockefeller officials also were fascinated with the promise of psychiatry and, ignoring criticism from some quarters, had been aligning themselves with German psychiatrists of all stripes. Abraham Flexner was instrumental in helping to fund the Kaiser Wilhelm Institute for Psychiatry in Munich during its organizational phases. As early as 1903, its director Ernst Rudin argued that alcoholism was an inherited trait and that alcoholics should be segregated and not be permitted to marry unless they first were sterilized. Rudin was admired by many American colleagues and his research widely reported in leading medical journals. Later he would become the architect of Nazi Germany's racially based human experimentations; Hitler congratulated him for being "a meritorious pioneer of the racial-hygiene measures of the Third Reich."

But by the 1930s (after Flexner's departure) enthusiasm for eugenics research by new Rockefeller leaders began to wane. In November, 1932 when Professor Rudin wrote to Lawrence Dunham, director of the Bureau of Social Hygiene requesting continuing support of Kaiser Wilhelm Institute projects, he noted how when he'd visited a few years earlier, the leaders had been "sympathetic towards studies in eugenics and allied fields of research in heredity prognosis."[12] However, this time the money was not forthcoming. That same year Harry Laughlin requested support for an exhibition at an international eugenics congress, that "will bring together…the facts and studies which at present underlie the technique by which family-stocks, races and nations can influence their own trends in hereditary constitution." The request was denied and over the next few years, Rockefeller support for eugenics organizations was gradually scaled back.

In his biography of Simon Flexner, James Thomas Flexner noted that his father subscribed in the economics sphere to the Darwinian doctrine of the survival of the fittest:

> Simon felt that he was enabled by the Rockefeller fortune to liberate human beings through knocking off shackles of illness and fostering institutions that gave the humbly born ladders which, if they had the ability, they could climb. Although deeply involved with health measures that would help populations in the mass, he

felt no special responsibility for the mediocre, the stupid or the improvident. Self-made Simon did not share the theoretical sympathy which delicately nurtured Helen [his wife] felt for liberal and even radical causes. But he found it much easier to make peace with the rough and tumble of the world.[13]

Such circumstantial evidence does not establish that either Simon or Abe personally endorsed eugenics theory or practice, but as in many other areas, there could be discrepancies between Abraham Flexner's words and his actions. Whatever their true feelings may have been, the brothers were members of the American Eugenics Society, a large organization whose proselytizing during the 1920s accounted for a majority of high school biology texts endorsing eugenics. In 1930 *Eugenical News* reported that the Flexners helped organize an eightieth birthday celebration for Dr. William Welch who had served as Chairman of the Scientific Board of the Eugenics Record Office from 1913 to 1918. Simon chaired the event and Abraham served on the executive committee along with Harvey Cushing and John D. Rockefeller, Jr.[14]

Reluctant as I am to engage in guilt by association, it's hard to ignore the fact that among the most fervent supporters of eugenics theory was the Flexner brother's colleague at Rockefeller, the Nobel Prize winning surgeon Alexis Carrel whom Abraham later would appoint as a trustee of the IAS. Dr. Carrel who had radical views about social issues once told the *New York Times*,

There is no escaping the fact that men are not created equal...the fallacy of equality was invented in the eighteenth century when there was no science to correct it....Society must identify and encourage those with greatest ability, while the dregs should be disposed of in small euthanistic institutions supplied with the proper gases. Why preserve useless and harmful beings?" The work of creating useful beings should be directed by a "high council of experts" living in seclusion like monks – "audacious men of science, unafraid of resorting to extreme, even ruthless measures.[15]

Alexis Carrel proposed "lethal chambers" for the unfit and praised eugenics policies in the Third Reich: "The German government has taken energetic measures against the propagation of the defective, the mentally diseased and the criminal. The ideal solution would be the suppression of these individuals as soon as he has proven himself to be dangerous." Dr. Carrel elaborated his social prescriptions in *Man, the Unknown*, which in 1936 was the year's top-selling book, second overall only to the novel *Gone With The Wind*. That same year his face appeared on the cover of *Time* Magazine in company with Benito Mussolini, Douglas MacArthur and J.Edgar Hoover. During the War he formed a Foundation for the Vichy Government which pursued race-based research, but because he died in November, 1944 this activity was not prosecuted.

In 1930 Abraham Flexner was introduced to the aviation hero Charles Lindbergh who was working with Alexis Carrel at the Rockefeller Institute on a prototype extracorporeal heart by-pass pump. Later, Lindbergh came to rely on Flexner as his principal adviser in the charitable disposition of his New Jersey estate after the famous kidnapping of his young son. Lindbergh was anti-Semitic, a white supremacist and an anti-war activist. In 1941 Flexner reluctantly turned against his friend writing, "I am sorry about Lindbergh for he has ruined his life. He is a nice boy whom I know well, but he is uneducated and was completely taken in [by the Nazis]...After the kidnapping of his child he sought my advice – a Jew."[16] The source of their dispute apparently related to their differing opinions about war with Flexner having nothing to say about Lindbergh's other ideas.

So how can we reconcile, Flexner's words to the social workers in 1928 that race-based theories were "nonsense" with his close associations with the likes of Pritchett, Elliot, Poll, Carrel, Lindbergh and many other eugenicists? Did he ever dispute them, or was it more comfortable for him to accommodate?

Although there is no evidence that Flexner approved of "negative" eugenics and even if he might have been obtuse about some of the ethical implications, an important distinction between his vision of an intellectual elite and pure eugenics ideology was that he believed individuals were *not* indelibly rendered "unfit" by their heredity -- they could be improved, up to a point, through education.

Neither a racist nor a bigot, he insisted that the educational system in a democratic society needed to be removed from "shackles of poverty, race, color, every possible biological accident and social prejudice." As he saw it, the purpose of the American system of education was "to promote and to take advantage of social plasticity" by looking to the "reassignment of the individual on his own merits."

Concerning the crucial role of foundations as social managers in a democracy, Flexner declared that "the soundness of reform can never be left to the mercy of majority vote, else the human race would still be in the state of cave men...votes must be weighed not counted."[17] He wrote in *I Remember* that a danger of democracy is that "it will fail to appreciate excellence, for in very truth an aristocracy of excellence is the truest form of democracy."[18] A caveat was that the children of the well-to-do should be judged by precisely the same standards as are applied to the children of the poor – in effect, an intellectual meritocracy. His favored approach was to select a few able students for advanced education who would become leaders of the masses of men. There should be access for all to the highest standards of education, but no watering down to accommodate everyone.[19]

However, even if Flexner eschewed hereditarian aspects of eugenics theory, in some respects the effects of his brand of elitism were much the same. As Stephen Jay Gould observed in *The Mismeasure of Man* when discussing intelligence testing:

> One cannot attribute these conclusions to some mysterious "temper of the times" for contemporary critics saw through the nonsense as well. Even by standards of their own era, the American hereditarians were dogmatists but their dogma wafted up on favorable currents into realms of general acceptance with tragic consequences.[20]

Abraham Flexner may not have been a hereditarian, but surely he was a dogmatist who sincerely believed that social welfare could be accomplished through enlightened and beneficent supervision by a meritocracy. The intent of such a philosophy may have been admirable, but it would prove to be naïve.

THE INSTITUTE

Having completed a two month stint at Oxford, for the remainder of 1928 and much of the next year Flexner retraced his earlier steps across Europe. He visited universities, renewed friendships and considered new options. He was pleased to learn that the medical faculty in Berlin had voted to give him an honorary degree in medicine -- as the dean said, "no discussion of medical education now takes place that does not start from the exposition of your views."[1]

While in Germany he expressed concern about the growing number of anti-Semitic incidents and after attending a concert by the violin prodigy Yehudi Menuhin, uncharacteristically wrote to his wife, "I was glad that he was an American, that he was a Jew."[2] The aging curmudgeon was in relatively good health, still was ambitious and then, once again, opportunity came knocking in an unusual way – this time rather than seeking out money, it sought him.

Louis Bamberger (1855-1944) was a shy man who seldom spoke in public and never married. A high school drop-out at age fourteen, he'd moved from Baltimore to Newark in 1892 where he bought a bankrupt dry goods shop with his close friend (and soon to be brother-in-law) Felix H. Fuld. They turned it into the nation's fourth largest retail store doing $35 million of business a year. Bamberger and Felix and Caroline Fuld were virtually inseparable living together on a thirty-three acre estate which straddled the border of Newark and South Orange. When Felix Fuld died in January 1929, Louis felt unable to carry on alone and with his sister decided to sell the business and devote their remaining time to philanthropy.

R.H.Macy purchased their store for $25 million just six weeks before the stock-market crashed in October 1929. $1 million in cash or annuities was distributed to long-time executives and employees and there being no heirs, the siblings wished to return the rest of their fortune to the city and state which had benefited them in many ways. They had supported various civic projects, particularly Jewish institutions like Newark's Beth Israel Hospital and the YMHA, and now considered earmarking $5 million to build a medical school on their joint estate (in time, their contributions would exceed $15 million.) Perceiving that there was anti-Semitic prejudice in the medical establishment, they wished to favor Jewish applicants in their school. Two of Bamberger's trusted advisors, Herbert Maass and Samuel Leidesdorf had concerns about the project's feasibility and in late 1929 they decided to consult with the most influential figure in American medical education, Abraham Flexner. His advice was not what they expected.

As Flexner later described in his memoirs, "I was working quietly [in his office at the Rockefeller Institute provided by his brother] one day when the telephone rang and I was asked to see two gentlemen who wished to discuss with me the possible uses to which a considerable sum of money might be placed." After they elaborated on the Bamberger plan, Flexner scoffed at the visitor's concern about anti-Semitic prejudice in enlightened American medical schools. The wrong way to counter anti-Semitism would be to set up institutions favoring Jews – genius should be the only appointment criterion. Moreover, in his opinion there already were too many medical schools and too many physicians, especially in the northeast.

Then Flexner challenged the emissaries by asking, "Have you ever dreamed a dream?" Scarcely waiting for an answer, he proceeded to describe his own vision of a purely graduate university, an American community of "men and women of genius, of unusual talent, and of high devotion." Their research would be driven by their own curiosity and not burdened by teaching or administrative responsibilities.

Although Flexner admired European scholarship, the new Institute he envisioned would have a distinct American character similar to what Gilman had achieved at Johns Hopkins. Also it should resemble the Rockefeller Institute which in the field of medical research had been developed by his brother Simon. It would be "a paradise for scholars" where everyone endeavored to advance the frontiers of knowledge -- no students, no classes and no degrees.

Flexner gave proofs of his new book *University Education, American, English and German* for Maass and Leidesdorf to read; they were impressed and the Bamberger siblings soon were persuaded, but it was not until long after the donors were fully committed that Flexner dissuaded them from their intention to place the enterprise on their South Orange estate. A first-rate graduate school should be associated with a leading university and library, neither of which existed in Newark, but Princeton would be an ideal location in New Jersey.

In his autobiography Flexner recalled how at age 63 he had been reluctant to accept the Founder's request that he head the project, but was persuaded by his wife who said, "You will have to do it. You have spent your life criticizing other people. You can't refuse to give them a chance to criticize you."[3] As Bonner described, it was "Flexner's triumphant return to the limelight after his no-holds barred attack on American universities" He was determined to move carefully: "I haven't a conviction that I am not willing to sacrifice because I want to do the thing right."

The Institute was officially incorporated on May 30, 1930 with Louis Bamberger and Mrs. Felix Fuld heading the Board of Trustees. From Flexner's viewpoint, "It is our prime and essential function to develop an American culture and civilization...comparable in value to those of the Western European countries."

It would be the first in America where "young men and women could continue independent training beyond the Ph.D. degree without pressure of numbers or routine: "I shall seek a few first-rate men and give them ample salaries on condition they hold up their end of the job." Flexner explained, "I am not unaware of the fact that I have sketched an educational Utopia. I have deliberately hitched the Institute to a star; it would be wrong to begin with any other ambition or aspiration."

At the first Trustees meeting in September, 1931 he expanded on the grand design for this "fortress of learning."

> The Institute for Advanced Study will be neither a current university struggling with diverse tasks and many students, nor a research institute, devoted solely to the solution of problems. It may be pictured as a wedge inserted between the two...I should think of a circle...within this, I should, one by one, as men and funds are available – and only then – create a series of schools or groups – a school of mathematics, a school of economics, a school of history, a school of philosophy, etc. The "schools" may change from time to time; in any event, the designations are so broad that they may readily cover one group of activities today, quite another group as time goes on...Each school should conduct its affairs in its own way for neither the subjects nor the scholars will all fit into one mould.[4]

Flexner charged the celebrated Princeton mathematician Oswald Veblan with recruiting the best and brightest to this scientific Camelot.They would be provided a place for study where they could "teach best by not teaching at all," where there would be "no duties, only opportunities." Mathematics was a favored discipline partially because all that was needed was a blackboard and chalk, paper and pencils -- when Einstein arrived, he also requested a large waste basket: "so I can throw away all my mistakes."[5] More important, there already were a number of brilliant mathematicians at Princeton and a new building was being planned to accommodate them.

The Institute didn't officially open its doors until October 2, 1933 on land donated by the university. Among the brilliant cadre assembled was the charismatic Hungarian John von Neuman, later described as "the father of the computer." He found Princeton's sylvan setting a bit too serene for his cosmopolitan taste, lacking the intellectual stimulation afforded in European coffee houses. However, von Neuman acknowledged that if civilization was to survive it would have to be in America.[6]

During the 1930s, because of harsh new American immigration policies, Jewish refugees desperately sought other ports of call. More than 1,500 scientists, sometimes described as "Hitler's Gift," fled to England; twenty of them went on to win Nobel Prizes. Ernst Boris Chain, a co-discover of Penicillin, recalled that with the Nazi ascendancy, "Europe was temporarily plunged into a darkness in which "the Middle Ages appear as a blaze of light."[7] Albert Einstein had been a deeply committed pacifist, but by 1933 was forced to change his mind: "Until recently we in Europe could assume that personal war resistance constituted an effective attack on militarism. Today we face an altogether different situation. In the heart of Europe lies a power in Germany that is obviously pushing to war with all available means."[8]

Einstein, who had been leading an itinerant life, once described himself as "a bird in passage." However, by 1929 the situation in Germany was becoming untenable and he considered invitations from Madrid, Leiden, Paris, Oxford and Turkey, among others. Robert Milliken of Caltech had been trying for years to lure the scientist to Pasadena on a permanent basis, but seeing an opportunity to seize the crown jewel for his new Institute, Flexner began a quiet but persistent courtship. Starting in California, he pursued his prey to Oxford and Europe where they negotiated terms. Thanks to the Bamberger largesse, Flexner was able to make a better offer than Caltech.

Although they came to a tentative agreement in 1932, Einstein continued to have reservations, including whether his coming to Princeton where the university was known to have a *numerus clausus* (quota) might be misconstrued as acquiescing with such a policy.[9] The Institute and the University were never formally united, but had close academic and intellectual relations, what Princeton's literature referred to as a "fortunate symbiosis." At the time only about two percent of Princeton University's freshman admissions and a smattering of faculty were Jewish. Einstein must have been sufficiently reassured, but once their agreement was sealed, Flexner worried that too bold or public a stance by his superstar in favor of Jewish refugees would stir up anti-Semitism. The Institute should be "a haven where scholars and scientists could regard the world and its phenomena as their laboratory without being carried off in the maelstrom of the immediate." He wrote to Herbert Maas, "Einstein...has done a number of foolish things since going to Europe. Of course, I do not allow them to disturb me in the least, for I know that, when he reaches Princeton, I shall contrive to manage him and his wife."[10]

Trouble flared up as soon as the Einsteins arrived in America on October 17, 1933. New York's mayor had prepared a gala welcome at the Battery, but Flexner arranged for the Einsteins to be taken off the ship at Quarantine Island in New York Harbor and directly hustled off to Princeton. The mayor, cheerleaders and a brass band were left waiting in the rain at the dock for the hero who never arrived. Flexner sent a note which was delivered to the Einsteins when they debarked cautioning that their safety in America depended upon silence and refraining from attendance at public functions: Flexner later contended that it was the Einsteins who wished to land secretly and he only had gone along out of concern for their physical safety. Whether or not the Einsteins were complicit in the ruse, Flexner's concern about their safety was genuine. Before coming to America, Einstein had been warned that the Nazis had put a price upon his head and that his life was not safe even outside Germany. In retrospect, Flexner may have been misguided in his fears, but what happened next, revealed the Director at his manipulative worst.

Two weeks after the Einsteins settled in, Rabbi Stephen Wise of New York arranged with President Roosevelt's social secretary for them to be invited to visit the White House. Rabbi Wise felt that FDR hadn't raised a finger to help the Jews of Germany and hoped this visit would help focus the President's attention on their plight. In turn the President needed a public symbol of his sympathy.

Roosevelt's social secretary called to arrange the details, but when Flexner found out he was furious. He called the White House directly, advising them that all invitations must go through him, and then refused the invitation. Flexner explained to FDR, "with his [Einstein's] consent and at his desire I have declined in his behalf invitations from high officials and from scientific societies in whose work he is really interested."

Einstein knew nothing about these machinations and when he did find out, hastened to contact Eleanor Roosevelt. This time the invitation was personally extended and the Einsteins visited on January 24, 1934, had dinner and spent the night. Einstein complained about the incident to Rabbi Wise in a letter in which he wrote as his return address "Concentration Camp, Princeton." In addition, he sent a five page letter to the Institute's trustees complaining of "constant interference of the type that no self-respecting person would tolerate." If Flexner continued this behavior, Einstein proposed "severing my relationship with your institute in a dignified manner." .

The Director backed off and, to give Flexner his due, justified his behavior on an informal discussion he claimed to have had with the Einsteins early in their negotiations when he felt they had been grateful for his solicitude in protecting them from unwanted publicity. He took this as blanket authorization to act in their behalf -- including intercepting and reading their mail. If an assassination attempt was a real possibility, the safest course would be to keep the naïve professor in seclusion where he could smoke his pipe, play his violin - and think. Flexner believed that the Einsteins had a penchant for publicity;

they occasionally appeared at events designed to raise money for Jewish refugees and he continued to council against it. Perturbed when they rejected his advice, in a revealing letter to Elsa Einstein he warned that if Jews got too much attention, it would stoke anti-Semitism:

> It is perfectly possible to create anti-Semitic feeling in the United States. There is no danger that any such feeling would be created *except by the Jews themselves*. (my italics) There are already signs which are unmistakable that anti-Semitism has increased in America. It is because I am myself a Jew and because I wish to help oppressed Jews in Germany that my efforts, though continuous and in a measure successful, are absolutely quiet and anonymous…The questions involved are the dignity of your husband and the Institute according to the highest American standards and the most effective way of helping the Jewish race in America and in Europe." [11]

Flexner's position seemed clear enough: Jews had brought misfortune upon themselves. In a separate letter to Albert Einstein that same day, again he argued that Jews should keep a low-profile: "I have felt this from the moment that Hitler began his anti-Jewish policy, and I have acted accordingly.…There have been indications in American universities that Jewish students and Jewish professors will suffer unless the utmost caution is used."[12] For his part, Einstein told Flexner, "In these times of danger to Jewish and liberal interests one is morally forced to take on many things that in normal times could be avoided."[13]

Less than one month after the Einsteins arrived in Princeton, Flexner wrote the following to Institute trustee Herbert Maass,

> I am beginning to weary a little of this daily necessity of 'sitting down' upon Einstein and his wife. They do not know America. They are the merest children, and they

are extremely difficult to advise and control. You have no idea of the barrage of publicity which I have intercepted. I should suppose that half my time is devoted to protecting Einstein. It will be worthwhile if I succeed in doing it permanently within this year. Otherwise, a very serious problem regarding Professor Einstein may arise.[14]

By December, 1933 AF wrote "the E's have broken their promise in almost every possible way and have brought down upon themselves very serious criticism, not only in Princeton but elsewhere."[15] Einstein would later dismiss the White House incident as "the little war in the beer glass."[16] In turn, Flexner reported to Bamberger that Einstein was happy, "all the little misunderstandings" had been removed and tranquility reigned,[17] However, a rift remained which soon would deepen and years later in a moment of candor, Einstein would refer to Flexner as one of his "few enemies" in Princeton.[18]

A postscript to this lamentable story concerns the attitude of many Princetonians toward Jews during the 1930s. In 1937 when the negro contralto Marian Anderson came to Princeton for a concert, she was refused a room at the Nassau Inn. Einstein invited her to stay at his little house at 112 Mercer Street and in later years whenever she returned, she'd stay with him. In 1938, the *New York Times* reported the result of a survey of incoming Princeton freshmen and for the second year in a row Adolf Hitler polled highest as the "greatest living person." Albert Einstein was second.[19]

END GAME

Abraham Flexner's problems in Princeton were only beginning. When Louis Bamberger had insisted upon including some of his intimates on the 15 member Board of Trustees, the Director had been untroubled since he was confident in his powers of diplomacy, flattery and persuasion. Flexner's strategy apparently was to keep the trustees informed at Board meetings; in effect, they would be reduced to rubber-stamping his policies. Included as window dressing were the Nobel Prize winner Alexis Carrel and New York's lieutenant governor Herbert Lehman, but a later appointment who would prove to be especially troublesome was the combative Harvard Law professor Felix Frankfurter.

The future Supreme Court justice argued that Flexner should "get Europe out of his system", that American models should be followed and emphasis placed on social sciences rather than on mathematics. Moreover, despite Flexner's writings and honorary degrees, Frankfurter considered his scholarly qualifications to be wanting. In a nasty exchange of letters Flexner objected to Frankfurter's having characterized German universities as "foci of so much moral poison for the world both in the 19th and 20th century." According to Flexner:

> It would be just as fair to speak of Harvard, Yale, Columbia and Chicago as being poisonous *foci*, because of their business schools or snobbishness or schools of journalism…Think for a moment! The German

universities were the most powerful influence in the 19th century that operated to elevate higher education in the United States. Without them there would have been no Johns Hopkins University or Medical School, and without the Johns Hopkins University and Medical School, how much farther back we would have been! [1]

Frankfurter found it "difficult to penetrate [Flexner's] thick skin" and their disagreements would escalate.[2] The director considered the professor to be a "troublemaker" and when Frankfurter could not be intimidated, threatened to resign if he were reappointed as a trustee: "They shall have to choose between us."[3] As it turned out, Flexner won that battle, but would lose the war. Just as had transpired a decade earlier at the GEB, Flexner's domineering style created conflict. His premise was to keep the distinguished faculty out of administrative matters because, inevitably, it would lead to bickering and backbiting and in this he proved to be correct.

As time passed Flexner was less willing to receive advice and faculty members grew impatient with what they perceived as his pettiness, meddling and occasional bad judgment. There was tension over salaries, pensions, budgets, hiring practices, office space and even parking. The issue of anti-Semitism at the university continued to simmer, but Flexner refused to be drawn into these discussions lest it compromise his standing with Princeton's President Dodds. As noted in Steve Batterson's book *Pursuit of Genius* about the early years of the IAS, Flexner considered the anti-Semitism issue at Princeton as "the third rail for the relations he was cultivating."[4] Complaints became more rancorous and he justified his aversion to faculty meetings insisting that it was in their best interest:

Academic democracy means letting men of brains alone – and this can be achieved only if the head (president, director, or whatever he is called), has tact and good sense enough to confer with the proper people and dispose of current affairs in the general interest. He will be called an autocrat – but how can he be if individuals are free to follow their own bent and are not distracted by the routine of "talk fests" such as committee and faculty meetings inevitably become.[5]

Abraham Flexner now was 72 years old and, as he had before at Rockefeller, began to hint about retirement; however, he was vague about when. Those dissidents who wanted to force the issue argued that he no longer was able to handle the demands of running the Institute, but the Director stood between them and the Board and a majority of the trustees would be needed to oppose reappointment. Several of the faculty reached out to Board members who might be sympathetic. They targeted Herbert Maass and Samuel Leidesdorf who in 1930 had been Bamberger's emissaries to whom Flexner denied that anti-Semitism was a significant issue in American universities and medical schools.

By 1937, these two both had sons who'd recently been turned down for college admission, Maass' son at Princeton. When the trustees asked him about anti-Semitism in the Princeton community and expressed fear that someday the Institute itself might be susceptible, once again, he lectured them that enlightenment and discrimination were incompatible -- not only at Princeton but at other universities. They remained unconvinced and the issue reemerged in January, 1938 when at a Board meeting, and without specifically mentioning Judaism or anti-Semitism, Flexner digressed from the agenda to discuss the extent of religious and racial prejudice generally:

I have myself no fear for the future of American universities….Faculties, and I speak from a wide and intimate acquaintance with them in all sections of the country – have practically without exception long since risen above denominational or racial prejudice, but as a matter of fact decisions unfavorable to this or that person are often based upon merely the enforcement of high standards, and it is frequently a face-saving gesture on the part of the unfortunate individual to attribute his ill success to intolerance.[6]

Whether or not intended as a personal reference, it was insensitive and both Maass and Leidesdorf were deeply offended. They took Flexner's remarks as unmistakable reference to their own son's experiences and from this point their sympathies in the faculty revolt shifted against the Director. Flexner stonewalled more direct requests for him to retire and felt that he was performing his duties in an exceptional manner.

Oblivious to appeals by his wife, brother and friends to retire gracefully, he heard only what he wanted to hear. At times AF would speak of the welcome freedom that retirement would provide, but if such sentiment was real, it was outweighed by the humiliation of being forced out -- for a second time. He tried to gain support from Board members and sought an exit strategy which could not be construed by anyone as capitulation to his enemies.[7]

Flexner's most formidable adversary during this prolonged end-game was the mathematician Oswald Veblen (1880-1960.) The nephew of famed Norwegian-American social theorist Thorsten Veblen had come to Princeton in 1905 and would remain there for more than five decades. Veblen was as equally determined as Flexner to have his way and as early as 1924 had proposed a mathematics institute where research rather than teaching would be the primary business. Veblen's dream, like Flexner's, was to develop a community of scholars at Princeton similar to some that he had observed in Europe. Princeton's mathematics department already stood with Harvard as the nation's finest and although lack of physical space had been a problem, Veblen and others had successfully raised money to build a fairly lavish building, Fine Hall (which opened in 1931.)

During the 1920s, Oswald Veblen sought to have development funds for his mathematics institute added to a larger grant package which Princeton was submitting to the GEB where Flexner still was a key figure. Although the university received a sizable grant, the mathematics request was deleted. In 1930 Veblen read a newspaper account of the Bamberger's intention to establish a research institute in Newark and wrote a congratulatory message to Flexner which proposed Princeton as a better site. Flexner agreed and the two men's dreams converged, Veblen became Flexner's most influential advisor and persuaded him to begin by concentrating on mathematics since Princeton already had an outstanding faculty and soon would have a brand new building.

One of Flexner's core beliefs was that undergraduate and graduate education were incompatible, but Veblen was committed to predoctoral teaching. While Flexner's original intention had been to have only two or three scholars in each discipline; Veblen wanted more mathematicians and as financial exigencies increased during the 1930s, the Director was hard pressed to keep up with needs of the burgeoning department which soon swelled to five full-timers. It was inevitable that these two forceful men with rather different agendas would clash.

As the faculty coup evolved, Flexner blamed much of his trouble on Veblen whom he suspected as being the ring leader. Among many other things, he believed that Veblen had influenced Einstein by warning that the Director's deficit spending would imperil pension benefits. But perhaps the most persistent faculty critic was historian Edward M. Earle. On Veblen's advice he wrote a frank letter to the Director reiterating concerns that he and others had voiced repeatedly:

> You asked me yesterday that I tell you the truth without fear or favor. As a matter of fact, that is precisely what I have been trying to do in innumerable conversations during the past three years. I have expressed to you my alarm on a number of points; more specifically: your policies vis a vis Princeton University; your refusal to admit the presence of anti-Semitism in the community, your openly expressed contempt for fellow members of the faculty, sometimes taking the form of personal

abuse....your resistance to a measure of faculty participation in vital decisions, your refusal to transmit to the Trustees a respectful modest request for such participation [and] your procedure....I know from bitter experience that you do not welcome criticism, however friendly, which expresses disagreement with some of your policies and attitudes. What I – who owe you so much and who hold you in so deep an affection – feel and see is felt and seen in more marked degree by other members of the faculty...." [8]

That same day Professor Earle wrote to Frank Aydelotte:

It is all rather tragic that Flexner does not have the dignity and the courage to step out gracefully, but I suppose it was too much to expect that he would.... Won't it be a joy when this is all settled and we can get down to work once more?[9]

A week later Earle wrote to Veblen to bring him up to date:

I do not need to tell you that allowing Abe to continue on any terms would be a major catastrophe. He will consider it a triumph over everyone concerned. It will give him an unparalleled opportunity to exercise his conspiratorial abilities. Even more it will give him control over the budget and other vital matters during the coming critical year for the Institute. No matter how good our case on its merits, however, there is no assurance that it will triumph over the timidity of Maass and Leidesdorf. They are the crucial people, and I write to ask you to consider what measures had best be taken....Einstein indicated to me the day I drove him into New York that he would not be disposed to continue at the Institute if action were not taken on A.F. at this time.

Do you think it would be wise to request Einstein to bring further pressure to bear at this time? In any case something must be done. (July 13, 1939)[10]

Bonner suggests that the faculty were unduly harsh in their indictments, that they could not have known the severe limitations under which Flexner worked, the ambiguity of the donors over finances, the institute's dependence on the university's good will and mixed messages he had received from various insiders. Nevertheless, two weeks later Edward Earle explained to trustee Herbert Maass (July 26, 1939):

I have known him [A.F.] for almost fifteen years, for most of which time he has been almost a father to me and I have truly loved him. He has always been kindly, considerate, and straight-forward. During the last two years, however, he has become increasingly hostile to the most friendly advice and criticism and has been so abusive toward those who offer it that it has seemed that friendship with him could be preserved only by becoming a "yes man", which to most of us is altogether repulsive. He has developed all sorts of eccentricities which make it exceedingly difficult to transact business with him. Most serious of all, however, is his ability at self-deception; this makes him so untruthful that none of us can trust him in the smallest detail. He has lost his grip on the affairs of the Institute and is altogether unable, I believe, to handle the details which will go with our occupancy of the new building....In view of his long record of distinction in his work and of kindliness in his personal relationships, this change in him can only be accounted for by his age; as I have told you, one of his physicians told me that he has shown definite medical signs of senility.[11]

Professor Earle, seemingly still conflicted, went on to describe how sometimes a "dutiful son" must provide tough love:

> It is because I am still devoted to Dr. Flexner that I wish to avoid the public scandal which is almost certain to occur if he continues another year as director – a scandal which may destroy his professional and personal reputation, be disastrous to the Institute and may be the greatest possible unkindness to those sweet and kindly people Mr. Bamberger and Mrs. Fuld...My conscience is altogether clear as to the course I have chosen. It would have been easier for me personally to keep still, draw my salary, do a minimum of work and let events take their course. That, however, is not my conception of loyalty to Dr. Flexner.

In truth the issue of Flexner's health had become an issue and if not senile, he was feeling weary, depressed and betrayed. On August 12, 1939, unable to hold out any longer, he sent letters to the trustees informing them of his intention to resign as of the October Board meeting. To Professor Earle he wrote, "I have been seeking retirement for the last two or three years and I have postponed it in deference to the wishes of Mr. Bamberger and Mrs. Fuld. I am retiring now with their consent and of my own volition."[12] No doubt there was a collective sigh of relief. A newspaper account reported that the Director had resigned "for reasons of health, his physician having advised him to avoid all stress and strain."

Professor Earl explained things quite differently in a letter to David Mittrany, a faculty member of the Institute's School of Economics and Politics, who was one of the leading co-conspirators:

> One of the difficulties is that we all feel obliged to write him some sort of letter. If we make it laudatory, he quotes it to others as an example of the injustice of his

resignation. If otherwise, it is an example of ingratitude. I have written a kind of diplomatic masterpiece, the effect of which I do not yet know. I presume you will have to do likewise.[13]

Mittrany had had a stormy relationship with Flexner and earlier wrote to Earle that he blamed himself for allowing things to have reached such an impasse:

It is so much more difficult for you and me who have been personal friends; and though his conduct toward me has been unspeakable, it turns me sick to think of so many fine qualities so misused, and of his second great opportunity ending like the first in bitterness to himself and to his family.....It was obvious that matters were getting from bad to worse, and it would have been a service to all, not the least to Abe himself, to have prevented them from reaching this awful stage.[14]

The trustees and faculty all signed a statement expressing their indebtedness to the Director: "Whatever prestige the Institute enjoys or will enjoy in the future will be based upon the foundations established by Abraham Flexner." But before leaving Princeton, Flexner gave this parting advice to his close friend and successor Frank Aydelotte:

Don't for your own sake and that of the Institute underestimate the fact that you are dealing with ingrates. I freely confess that I was a baby in their hands....They wanted opportunities for scholarship, with high salaries, but they also wanted managerial and executive power.... You will have to make them....realize from the jump that you are the master.[15]

Abraham Flexner's style of revenge was predictable – the silent treatment; his memoirs barely mentioned Veblen at all. In the 1940 version his name appeared only once when describing how when famed mathematician Professor Weyl was recruited from Gottingen, "he joined us, *as did also Veblen....*" The 1960 update was barely more forthcoming: "he joined us, *as did Oswald Veblen, a professor at Princeton University....*" (my italics.) In 1960 when Professor Veblen died at age eighty (about one year after Flexner's death) the Institute's faculty and trustees provided vindication by acknowledging his great influence in developing it as a center for postdoctoral research:

> He loved simplicity and disliked sham. He placed the Institute ahead of his personal convenience. He possessed the art of friendship, and his assistance was decisive for the careers of dozens of men...We are grateful for his great strength and courage, for his unusual wisdom, for his unflinching integrity and honesty, for his uncompromising ideals and, not least, for his generous friendship.[16]

An obituary written by Deane Montgomery, then President of the American Mathematical Society, discretely acknowledged earlier conflicts – almost certainly referring to the Institute's first Director:

> Although Veblen had far more friends and admirers than most other men, it was of course inevitable that there was occasional friction with those who either did not understand or who found it expedient not to follow his shining academic ideals. Anyone familiar with the academic scene knows that the pressures against quality are formidable, and that the battle for excellence has no end. Excuses for weakness and pettiness in academic matters are so familiar as to be trite and are usually presented under the pretense of one or another noble motive, but for Veblen there did not exist a valid excuse for a choice of anything but the best.[17]

Oswald Veblen was not the only trustee to receive Flexner's silent treatment; other dissidents also were deleted from the memoirs. In *I Remember* the name of Herbert Maass was not mentioned at all (Samuel Leidesdorf merited a single reference as a friend with whom AF once had luncheon.).They were referred to only as "two gentlemen" who had visited Flexner as representatives of Louis Bamberger and Mrs. Fuld to ask about the feasibility of a medical school in Newark.[18]

Maass and Leidesdorf had sent a congratulatory telegram to Flexner on the Institute's opening day in 1933 extending "heartfelt congratulations upon the achievement of one of your life's dreams…We are proud and delighted to have been associated with you in its establishment…" But now having been omitted from Flexner's memoir, Herbert Maass felt compelled to set the record straight in his own unpublished history of the Institute's founding:

> Here I undertake to elaborate upon the record of history as contained in a book titled "I Remember", in which the author apparently forgot the genesis of his connection with the Institute for Advanced Study. Had it not been for the intensive interest evinced by Mr. Leidesdorf and me and the influence which we wielded with Mr. Bamberger and Mrs. Fuld, there may never have been such an Institute despite Dr. Flexner, his brilliant ideas and his appealing personality.[19]

In *I Remember* Abraham Flexner summed up: "The Institute was conceived as a paradise for scholars and such it really is. But not all men – not all gifted men – know how to live in paradise."[20] And what happened to "paradise" itself? According to a New York Times book review:

> There are no observatories or laboratories at the Institute – no telescopes, no test tubes, none of the clutter of experimental science. Nor are there any teachers, students or classrooms. There is virtually nothing to

distract anyone from the life of the mind. Members do not have to worry about money (the place has been called "the Institute for Advanced Salaries").They are not even obliged to talk to one another, and many of them don't...At any one time, some 200 people are thinking there. Most of them are temporary members, stellar young scholars on one-or two year stints. About 25 of the 200 are the permanent members who often choose to stay at the institute until they die. Why leave Platonic heaven?[21]

FLEXNER'S JEWISH
IDENTITY PROBLEM

In order to better understand Abraham Flexner's attitude about anti-Semitism in America, it may be helpful to consider his religious roots. The Flexners were descended from several generations of Moravian rabbis and, as already has been described, they led a familiar Jewish immigrant story: the parents devout, and the children less interested in ritual and determined to blend into the American mainstream. In Louisville Moritz Flexner continued to don phylacteries for morning prayer, as prescribed by traditional Jewish law; his wife lit Sabbath candles and often quoted Yiddish proverbs. In his memoirs Abraham recalled his parents with great respect and marveled at their self reliance and the "spiritual force" which sustained them through difficult times:

> At an early age...we began to be affected by the rationalistic spirit of the time. Our parents remained to the end of their lives pious Hebrews, attending synagogue regularly and observing religious feasts. They saw us drift away into streams of thought and feeling that they did not understand. They interposed no resistance. For us, Darwin, Herbert Spencer and Huxley, then at the height of their fame and influence, replaced the Bible and the prayer book; never a word of remonstrance,

inquiry, or expostulation escaped our parents. They were shrewd enough to realize that their hold upon their children was strengthened by the fact that they held them with a loose rein...They made our friends from a world alien to them, welcome in our home and at our table. It did not trouble my mother later that two of her sons [Abraham and Simon] married Christian girls.[1]

Louisville's German-Jewish community was adopting the changes of the liberal Reform movement and as Abe approached Bar Mitzvah age, an occasional visitor to the Flexner home was a young local rabbi Dr. Emil Hirsch. He was modern, a graduate of the University of Pennsylvania, and enjoyed arguing with the oldest son Jacob, who like many Americans of that time was intrigued by the philosophy of the agnostic Englishman Herbert Spencer. Emil's father Samuel Hirsch was one of the founders of Classical Reform Judaism in Germany and following in his footsteps, the son also was committed to social justice. Later in his career Emil Hirsch would be described as "the Jewish apostle to the non-Jewish world." Denying that Jews were a "chosen people," he taught that the Jewish mission was not to stand apart but to gather in all others, uniting mankind in righteousness and peace -- a person from whatever background was a Jew if he believed.

No doubt such universalist ideas impressed young Flexner minds and as they grew older, both Abraham and Simon came to consider themselves as not in any true sense Jewish. Not necessarily ashamed of being born Jewish, and never denying it, they took no special pride in it either. In order to harmonize with American society they felt obliged to shed the old ways and take on the trappings and attitudes of the dominant culture.[2] In his memoirs, Abraham Flexner acknowledged a Christian theologian, the 19th century French philosopher Ernest Renan as an important influence. Flexner cited the following passage from Renan's *Life of Jesus* which described a conversation of the woman of Samaria with Jesus:

"Our fathers worshipped in this mountain, and ye say that in Jerusalem is the place where men ought to worship." Jesus replied, "Woman, believe me, the hour cometh when we shall neither in this mountain, nor yet at Jerusalem, worship the Father, but when the true worshippers shall worship the Father in spirit and in truth."[3]

Perhaps the passage appealed to Abe as affirmation that true religion is love and that religious particulars are irrelevant. As he recalled more than a half century later, "It is, I think, no exaggeration to say that Renan's skillful use of this conversation quieted my religious doubts, and from that day to this my religious beliefs have traveled no further." Once when Reverend Harry Fosdick contended that religion was a way to bring meaning to "the chaos of good and bad," Flexner responded that religion was "organized human cowardice, a spiritual cocktail analogous to the drink a tired and harassed business man takes before dinner to mellow himself."[4]

In January, 1944 a young Jewish soldier who was contemplating conversion wrote Flexner for advice. The response was candid and personal, Flexner explaining "why Jewish faith was acceptable to my father and not to me."

I very early in my life ceased to believe that the Jews were the chosen people in the sense in which the orthodox Jews believed the words. I found out through my reading and through my studies at college that all churches and faiths have been made by men and are not inspired by God. In the early books of the Bible the Jews are a nomadic and often a cruel race, of whom God could not possibly have approved. I found as I matured, that people of other faiths had at times been equally cruel, that good people were by no means limited to the Jewish people...There are intolerant and ignorant Jews and the same kind of people are found among every religious denomination.

I would not for the world undermine your faith. On the other hand, you have asked me a direct question and I have given you an honest answer. We are seeing in the world today what evil things intolerant action and intolerant beliefs can bring about. The lesson of this war is tolerance, freedom of opinion, freedom of thought, freedom of speech and that terrible sacrifices that we are making and that you are prepared as an individual to make will, I hope, bring about the establishment of a world in which men and women will be judged as individuals regardless of faith, regardless of race, regardless of any of the accidents which surround us all at birth. [5]

If tolerance was a core lesson to be learned, Abraham Flexner sometimes failed to demonstrate that quality in his own behavior. At about the same time as the above letter, Edward Earle wrote to the Jewish trustees Maass and Leidesdorf to describe an incident when a distinguished young economist by the name of Weinberg had applied for an appointment to the IAS:

I was amazed to have Dr. Flexner throw cold water on the program. And I was shocked to have him comment on the "undesirable" name of Dr. Weinberg; although this was done jocularly, it reflected in my opinion his sensitiveness concerning the anti-Semitism of Princeton; in any case, it is the sort of thing which should on no account be done in humor or otherwise. [6]

Flexner's boss at Rockefeller Henry Gates, who harbored ill feelings toward many Jewish contemporaries, once told Abe that in his entire life he had known only three Jews of "inflexible courage" and proceeded to name him and his brother Simon as two of them. [7] In his character analysis of Abraham Flexner, Daniel Fox suggested that he fit the psychological description of an "exceptional Jew," one who was accepted as being unlike the rest and wished to defend their acceptance into polite society:

> Although Flexner preferred to ignore anti-Semitism, some of his aggressiveness, his delight in intellectual and bureaucratic combat, may have been a way to test his acceptance by Christian colleagues or a reaction to the stress of worrying about what was not said directly to him. His relative silence on the subject, when he was forthcoming on so many other matters, suggests that he was sensitive about it.[8]

His biographer Thomas Neville Bonner suggests that while working at the Rockefeller Foundation, Flexner may have suffered from "discrete anti-Semitism in the circles around him and felt he needed to continually prove himself." Depending upon the circumstances, Flexner might refer to his Jewish connection or entirely disengage. Shortly after resigning from the GEB, his commencement speech at the Training School for Jewish Social Workers in New York contained a rather ambiguous message. Speaking in the third person, he advised the graduates not only to become good Americans, but also to retain certain distinctive Jewish characteristics:

> In dealing with your specific problems you will need tact, insight, sympathy. For your real task is to substitute ties of one kind for another set of ties and in the process to save for American citizens all that is beautiful in the literary background of the Jewish communities in which you work.[9]

When Abraham Flexner sometimes spoke of his intimate knowledge that American universities had long since risen above denominational or racial prejudice, he was being disingenuous. If a man can be judged by his friends, consider his warm relationship with Yale's medical school Dean Milton Winternitz. The two first met in 1917 when Flexner agreed to help enlist the political support of Colonel Isaac Ullman, a Jewish tycoon who made his fortune manufacturing corsets, and now was the head of the Board of the New Haven Hospital. During their discussion, Flexner remarked, "I am a Jew myself and have been for years making my way among Christians and working with them...prejudice need not be stirred." In his memoirs Flexner recalled Milton Winternitz as "one of the most energetic, keen and able administrators that I encountered in the whole course of my dealings with medical schools." The Dean had only to ask and the GEB was quick to provide financial support.[10] For his part, Winternitz sometimes referred to Flexner as "Uncle Abe."[11]

Milton Winternitz was one of the first Jews to hold a major position of academic leadership. During his tenure as Dean of Yale Medical School from 1920 to 1935, he raised it from a second-rate institution to one of the finest in the world, modeled after Johns Hopkins. But as described by Dan Oren in *Joining the Club: A History of Jews at Yale*, the Dean was almost a caricature of a "self-hating"Jew striving to become part of gentile society.[12] Brilliant, charismatic, inspirational, he also was abusive and terrifying to students and faculty alike. He was variously described as "a genius," "a leader," "a bastard," "a sadistic brute," and "one of the worst anti-Semites I ever met." Judaism seemed to be a badge of shame for Winternitz. Although the Dean retained his surname, he preferred being called "Winter." Even his praise of Jewish colleagues could be backhanded; referring to one of them, "He certainly has none of the disagreeable qualities personally of his race."[13] Worse, in order to achieve a "balanced" class, Winternitz introduced a quota system at Yale, instructing the admissions committee, "Never admit more than five Jews, take only two Italian Catholics and take no blacks at all."

Ironically, at the same time that Abraham Flexner was organizing the Institute for Advanced Study at Princeton, Milton Winternitz was attempting to establish an Institute of Human Relations at Yale. His idea was to integrate humanistic studies such as history, philosophy and literature with scientific subjects so that patients would be studied as whole persons by well-rounded physicians. At first, the medical faculty was tolerant of the Dean's enthusiasm but in the aftermath of the Great Depression as money became tight, the very same men whom he'd recruited to Yale pushed back against these "wild ideas."

Yale's "Human Relations" venture failed largely because Winternitz suffered from the same dictatorial attitude as "Uncle Abe." A full scale faculty rebellion was mounted against him with the Board of Trustees siding with the faculty. According to one commentator: "Purely personal animosities and grudges were really the moving causes." Flexner also endorsed the concept of social medicine and proposed a major "Humanistic Foundation" at the IAS. Unlike Winternitz's failed advocacy of humanism in New Haven, the Institute for Advanced Studies at Princeton survived, but its founding Director was nudged out in the same way, and for much the same reason.

His father Moritz Flexner's emancipated generation had been forced to confront modernity in Europe, but in the new world their children were eager to be remodeled into Americans. Abe's conviction that Jews should not make waves was common among Jewish intellectuals of his era and during the first quarter of the 20th century leaders of the American Jewish Committee and B'nai B'rith sometimes warned that public outcries against anti-Semitic practices might be counterproductive. Indeed, in 1939 several prominent Jewish leaders urged President Roosevelt not to nominate Felix Frankfurter for the Supreme Court bench because they worried that having too many Jews on the court might fuel anti-Semitism.

Thomas Neville Bonner suggests that the Flexner brothers along with the likes of publisher Adolph Ochs, anthropologist Franz Boas, biologist Jacques Loeb and many others of their generation were secular Jews who through energy, industry and rectitude were successfully making their way in a strongly Christian culture. By shedding the religious habits of their parents and embracing the public schools they set out on the road to respectability and when anti-Semitism threatened it was best to pay no mind.[14]

An inclination not to call attention to their kind was evident even among some religious Jews. Typical was Rabbi Morris S. Lazaron (1888-1979) of Baltimore who was concerned about the allegation of anti-Semitic admissions policies in medical schools. In 1934 the rabbi wrote to the deans of 65 schools and directors of residency programs. Their responses confirmed discrimination with about 26 percent of Jewish applicants being accepted compared to 46 percent of Gentiles. There was wide variation according to location and most responders voiced opposition to any increase.

"Proportional representation" was a common justification but many respondents also expressed prejudicial remarks. One dean wrote that "the Jewish student does not have as high ethical standard as the average Christian student...he is more apt to be commercially inclined, and yet we have had exceptions to this general impression."[15] Others reported that while Jews were good at memorization or "book work," they lacked ability for practical work in the laboratory and wards.

Rabbi Lazaron advised accommodation to the system and counseled students to select alternate careers. Not only did he decide not to publish data which clearly illustrated discrimination, but in 1936 when a magazine publisher wished to publish his results, the rabbi explained:

> Publicity to the facts...has already been given through a number of the medical colleges in the country, and it an open question whether it would be advisable at the present time to make the material a matter of public discussion. Difficulties of the sort considered in the article can be much better solved through education in those quarters where education is necessary.[16]

Rabbi Lazaron was proud of his Sephardic heritage but also felt at home in the upper levels of gentile and Jewish society and counted various show business celebrities among his circle of friends. At the same time, many in the German-Jewish community (like the Flexners) whose ancestors had immigrated earlier than the hordes of Russian and Polish Jews, did not favor agitation. Their notion was that Jews were American like any other group and should not upset the apple cart -- better to keep your views to yourself.[17]

Conversely, Rabbi Stephen S. Wise filed a law suit to cancel Columbia University's tax exemption for violating a New York State anti-discrimination law. He argued that Columbia's College of Physicians and Surgeons had "betrayed the democratic purposes for which public subsidy for education is granted." At a public rally attended by Eleanor Roosevelt, Rabbi Wise denounced Columbia because of its "racially and religiously discriminatory practices." His petition was denied on technical grounds.

As the 1930s progressed and reports of Nazi intentions became better known, many who'd previously remained on the sidelines became more supportive of the Zionist cause. Among them was Abraham's younger brother Bernard Flexner who during World War I had been sent by the Red Cross to Romania where he saw the wretched conditions faced by many European Jews. He could not be indifferent to their problems and in 1919 volunteered to serve as legal counsel to the Zionist delegation at the Paris peace conference.

Later Bernard Flexner organized the Palestine Economic Corporation which was designed to promote land development, town planning, new industries and power development in Palestine. For his part, Abe considered brother Bernard's crusade to be quixotic: "For the life of me I cannot really believe that the creation of a Jewish state will achieve the good that is expected by the Zionists or that it will do the damage feared by those of a different mind."[18]

For decades there had been infighting between various Zionist factions and Bernard Flexner served as an intermediary between the warring parties when he reached out to a boyhood acquaintance, Supreme Court Justice Louis D. Brandeis who also had grown up in Louisville. Like the Flexners, Brandeis had a classical public education, did graduate studies in Germany and came from a family disconnected from its Jewish roots but dedicated to humanistic values. Brandeis even shared some of Abe's personal characteristics – elitism, intellectuality and reformist tendencies. But as the dismal outlook for German Jews became clearer, Brandeis felt the need to preserve "the spiritual legacy of Israel as an active force in the world." [19]

In March, 1933 when Rabbi Wise urged him to support public rallies in order to call attention to events in Germany, Brandeis responded, "Go ahead, and make the protest as good as you can." There should be no compromise nor negotiations with "supercautious" establishment Jews. To Brandeis' delight, on March 27 (seven months before Einstein's arrival in America) 22,000 people gathered in protest in Madison Square Garden while 30,000 more listened outside. The recruitment of Louis Brandeis was an important step for the Zionist cause because his social prestige made the movement respectable in the eyes of many American Jews. Not to Abraham Flexner.

Years later when Jacques Loeb was blackballed by the Century Club in New York, Flexner criticized a member who charged that the rejection stemmed from anti-Semitism. Flexner's reaction: "The fool has thus humiliated Loeb in the face of the town."[20] The message was clear enough: if anti-Semitism threatened, the best policy was to ignore it – "prejudice need not be stirred."

THE LAST DECADES

Although Edward Earle reported that doctors had suggested "senility" to account for Flexner's erratic behavior in Princeton, events of the next twenty years belied such a diagnosis. As his biographer Bonner noted, Flexner "did not go gently into the twilight years of his life."[1] After his unhappy retirement from the Institute for Advanced Study, the next two decades were bracketed by the autobiographies while during this same period he wrote three more books and consulted on various projects.

When conditions in Europe worsened during the 1930s, Flexner wrote that the world was going mad. Relatively early on he'd suggested that the English, French and Russians should smash Hitler and Mussolini before they got too strong. Never an isolationist or an appeaser, he criticized the weakness of Lloyd George, Neville Chamberlain and Joseph P. Kennedy and had little respect for FDR's early policies. He suggested that Rockefeller establish a fund to support German universities as a gesture of international good-will, but JDR, Jr. demurred. Now that war had broken out again, Abraham Flexner complained, "What I really want to do is to knock forty years off my age, shoulder my musket, and participate in the European war."[2]

Occasionally Flexner would make public speeches and seemed to enjoy the role of senior sage. Reflecting upon his long career:

From the day that I left Louisville to go to Baltimore, seventy-five years ago, I cannot see that I have pursued anything but an opportunistic course. I was not a philosopher. I had in my make-up something of a practical idealist.....I have been far too busy, and I have carried too heavy a weight of practical responsibility, to spend much time in subjective thinking. It is easy to see why I never stopped long enough to formulate a philosophy, but scanning critically opportunities as they turned up, seized avidly upon one after another....May the day never come when the prepared mind and the determined will may be halted by general considerations.[3]

More than two decades after his departure from the Rockefeller Foundation, Flexner invited Robert Calkins, then the director of the GEB, to lunch in order to complain about insufficient stress that was being placed on medical education. In describing the "tirade," Calkins wrote:

The best rule to follow with F, I have found, is to listen, say little, and never argue. F is wholly out of touch with scientific and educational developments and thinks the world is now just as it was when he was an officer of the Board. I have found no opportunity of convincing him otherwise and consequently have not argued the point with him."[4]

In 1952 Flexner published a small book *Funds and Foundations. Their policies past and present* and, true to form, used it as an opportunity to settle old scores. Still infuriated about how he'd been passed over in 1923 as director of the GEB but never mentioning that he'd coveted the position, he described the favored appointee Dr. Wickliffe Rose as "a great man...but great in what respect?" He then went on to describe how Rose previously was a "brilliant" sanitary administrator but had an unimpressive educational background and, worst of all, held different ideas about how the Board should be run. Rose hadn't appreciated that under Flexner's guidance the GEB had become "a university on a small scale...alive with ideas." An "invaluable tradition" which had been established now was in tatters, "entirely destroyed." In short, the selection of the "great" man was "disastrous."[5]

At the age of 74 Flexner became involved in a rancorous debate on the subject of preparing teachers and his tongue was as sharp as ever:

> I am no friend of teachers' colleges in the form that they have now assumed. They are absurd institutions, making no distinctions between what is significant and what is insignificant, admitting huge hordes of persons mostly without background, and usually without scholarly ambition, and undertaking by minute training in methods and statistics to produce a good teacher. The bad teaching that is so common in the United States is, in my judgment, in part due to the turn which teachers' colleges have taken in subordinating to training in technique the knowledge of the subject to be taught, and to the wire-pulling by which they have persuaded state and city boards of education to exact a certain number of hours of their training before anyone can become a "qualified" teacher or obtain promotion.[6]

Needless to say, this elicited a lively response. Still relishing a good fight, Flexner maintained: "We have to defend the country against mediocrity, mediocrity of soul, mediocrity of ideas, mediocrity of action. We must fight against it in ourselves." He complained that learning was becoming too passive and was skeptical about whether radio and television were good influences.[7]

Still interested in world affairs, in 1955 he wrote a letter to the *New York Times* comparing two speeches about American policy concerning Matsu and Quemoy, two small islands off the Chinese coast. He wrote that Adlai Stevenson made clear the "utter absurdity" of exaggerating their importance at the risk of nuclear war while debunking Secretary of State John Foster Dulles's declaration that "a craven peace" was worse than war.[8]

At age 82 Flexner took his own advice that "the best thing to do after retirement is to study" and enrolled as a freshman at Columbia University. For the next five years this sophisticated man who held numerous honorary degrees spent four hours a week auditing classes in Art History, American Literature and Russian History. When he refused having a 90th birthday party because it would interfere with his work, the remark drew admiring headlines, but he didn't decline a celebratory dinner at the Waldorf-Astoria Hotel for his contributions to medicine. The man who once was described as the severest critic and the best friend American medicine ever had was cheered by more than three hundred national leaders, including most of the deans of American medical schools.[9]

One speaker declared that Flexner had "made the greatest single contribution that [had] ever been made to the advancement of medical education in America." Another said that he'd spent his life fighting a "holy war against slackness, triviality and educational quackery." Dean Rusk, then president of the Rockefeller Foundation, remarked that during his fifteen years at the GEB, Flexner had exerted more direct influence over the course of medical and educational affairs in America than any other person in history. Rusk described his crucial qualities as "a burning ambition for excellence...the deep sympathy which expresses itself in candor – and not mere courtesy – contempt for pretense and fraud; a deep respect for an able mind wherever it is found; patience and persistence in the approach to perfection."[10]

Abraham Flexner died at his home in Falls Church, Virginia on September 21, 1959. Nearing age ninety-three, he'd recently completed his updated autobiography. One of the last visitors was his friend Allan Nevins who arranged posthumous publication of the sequel and wrote its introduction. In it he described Flexner as "one of the best talkers and listeners of his time, an omnivorous reader who delighted in the classics – imaginative, bold and a gifted organizer – yet a quiet, modest, dedicated man." Professor Nevins recalled the personality whom only his most intimate friends knew:

> His unfailing kindness and generosity, extended instinctively to everyone in any kind of need; his delightful wit and humor, always cheering, his quick discernment; his deep feeling for the beautiful in art and literature, and the just and accurate in science; his belief in self-sacrificing effort (which must also be hardheaded effort) for human betterment – these and other traits united to make his character as lovable as his accomplishments were impressive.[11]

Flexner's updated autobiography contained several new chapters but otherwise hardly differed from the first. Once again he recounted his personal triumphs and also described some of the good books that he'd read recently and the concerts and theatrical performances he'd attended. However, any attempt at self-analysis was superficial and self-serving. In the concluding chapter of both memoirs he summed up:

> As life goes, most people would call my career successful, and yet, if it is carefully examined, its interest does not lie in the novelty or originality of the things I have helped to do. I was quick to absorb, eager to execute. I got what I wanted in most cases because I reduced what I wanted to what I believed I could get, and in almost every case by the use of patience, persistence and good humor, things worked out well.....
> There is, I think, another aspect of my life that I cannot overlook; what am I? Myself? Not at all. I am what I have been made by association and contact with truly forceful men and women from whom I have gladly and eagerly learned from my fifteenth year to this very

day. I have been impressionable and selective.....At every stage in the writing of this book, I have thought of Carlyle' simple book plate, "I burn that I may be of use."[12]

In fairness, the conclusion of the updated autobiography did contain a wistful attempt at explanation:

Is there any incompatibility between the Utopia for scholars of which I have long dreamed and the "enthusiasm for the feasible" which spurred me on from day to day? I think not. Utopia in so far as humanly possible, can be realized only by trench warfare. Between Utopia, on the one hand, and the "feasible" on the other lies the no man's land, so well characterized by Browning as "The petty done, the undone past," which has to be conquered step by step. Of the undone vast" I am more keenly aware today than I was during the militant years of my activity. I had long had, to be sure, some sense of the gulf between the petty done and the undone vast in education in America and certain countries in Europe; but in other fields – industrial relations, social problems, racial contacts, art, and music -- I have only in relatively recent years become more and more acutely conscious.[13]

There was one revealing difference between the two autobiographies though --.the last page of the 1940 version had contained the following paragraph:

Unless society has been abominably governed over long periods, as was the case in Bourbon France and in czarist Russia, there is no danger that its control will fall for any great length of time into the hand of extremists. Meanwhile, we must not overlook the important role that the extremists play. They are a minority, but like Socrates and Jesus Christ, they are the gadflys that keep society from being too complacent or self-satisfied; they are, if sound, the spearhead of progress....If they are fundamentally wrong, free discussion will in time put an end to them. We have far more to fear from habit and conservatism, which are the natural results of growing years, than from relatively small and shifting bands of extremists. As the extremist grows older, he becomes more moderate.[14]

The words sounded splendid, but were strangely out of tune with the time. Perhaps it is uncharitable of me to suggest that Flexner's description of the constructive role "extremists" play in society may have contained an element of self-identity, even a hint of grandiosity. Far more important, consider what another "extremist" was doing in Germany that very same year of 1939 when Flexner was busy writing his autobiography.

Twenty years later, when composing the sequel, and considering all that had transpired during the ensuing decades, Flexner expressed no regret about his failure to anticipate the catastrophe that was about to overcome rationality and tolerance. Not that he could have done anything to prevent it but, even in retrospect, there was no remorse about how he might have been more prescient and proactive.

However, there was a subtle difference between the early and late memoirs, for in the updated version he altogether eliminated the paragraph about extremism. There can be no doubt that this was a calculated deletion; certainly not the act of a senile old man. This then was Abraham Flexner at his most irritating. The old "extremist" hadn't become more moderate at all. Apparently it was more comfortable to remain silent than to second guess himself.

JUDGING FLEXNER/
JUDGING A GENERATION

Without question Abraham Flexner left an indelible mark upon American education and the founding of the Institute of Advanced Study was a seminal event in intellectual history which indirectly led to nuclear energy and the computer. He wrote in *I Remember* that his gift was not original thinking but the ability to get things done, and what he got done was of the greatest significance.

If my characterization of him as being iconic as an education reformer may be overly generous, surely he was a legendary pathfinder. But we expect much from our icons and Flexner's narcissism was problematic and often worked against him. He fancied himself as an intellectual provocateur and it was difficult to be indifferent to him. He elicited conflicting adjectives: from his friends, "beloved brother," "gentle," "sweet," "lovable," "timid," "a practical jokester." Victims of his sarcastic criticism were more likely to describe him as "abrasive," "impatient," "uncompromising." John Gardner recalled no one ever called Abe "comfortable as an old shoe."[1]

As a power broker and fund raiser, Flexner could be persuasive, but as an administrator he was not an effective team player – gadflys rarely are. Perhaps his outwardly confident appearance reflected insecurity because of his lack of scholarly achievement or his Jewish background. Early in his career,

Flexner once wrote to his wife, "No one can ever know how high a price I pay for opportunity."[2] But he didn't elaborate about what price that was

If his memoirs were self-serving, there's no denying that his personal odyssey was inspiring – the outsider transformed into the ultimate insider. In his comprehensive review of Flexner's fifteen year tenure at the Rockefeller Foundation, Steven C. Wheatley addressing his inflexibility on policy and insensitivity to other people's feelings offered the following explanation:

> His history provides some clues to what is essentially a matter of psychological speculation. His success in the emerging philanthropic community had been based on the elegant simplicity of his ideas and their expression. Clarity, not ambiguity, was his stock-in-trade. That success had come late in life and must have been somewhat unexpected even to him. To have deviated from the formula which had served him so well would have required of him a tolerance for uncertainty which itself would have made his earlier achievements impossible. Moreover, his moralistic stress on the necessity of fidelity to academic ideals was no doubt reinforced by the displaced evangelicism and pietism which several scholars have noted as characteristics of the early Rockefeller boards. A habit of didactism may be another answer.
>
> Before coming to New York, he had spent his adult life almost entirely in the supervision of adolescents. He was perfectly comfortable in referring to negotiations with hospital and university trustees as "lessons" in which he was the patient but condescending instructor. In sum, it must be remembered that his life course was characterized by uncertainty: an unsteady father who never recovered from his failure in the Panic of 1877; a penurious childhood; the indeterminacy of his acceptance by a society which felt that anti-Semitism was only bad taste. His need to be self-assured must

have been too great for him ever to have considered the alternative.[3]

Wheatley's analysis rings true and the same pattern of behavior which Flexner displayed at the GEB continued during the Princeton decade; indeed, until the end of his life. As has been previously described, a paradox of Abraham Flexner's personality was how in educational affairs he could be such a fierce activist, while concerning certain issues outside of his direct sphere of influence he sometimes was uncharacteristically passive. When backed by wealthy tycoons on issues which they endorsed, he could afford to be fearless. But when his opinions ran contrary to the beliefs of his sponsors, it was prudent to be discrete -- if he did speak his mind, it was carefully calibrated so as not to compromise either himself or his employers.

Admittedly, to criticize an individual for failure to publicly take an unpopular stand on controversial subjects outside of his primary field of interest would require passing judgment upon many others of his generation who also chose to be silent observers. It was a time when, like him, many people trusted that intellect and civilized behavior would prevail and when many assimilated Jews felt that it was preferable to maintain a low profile.

In 1928 Flexner had publicly described eugenics theory as being "nonsense," but in his later writings there were no disavowals of race-based American immigration policies or coerced sterilizations of the "unfit" which were being espoused by some of his closest colleagues. Silences can be more telling than words and in Flexner's case there also were actions to account for since he was personally involved in providing Rockefeller support for early phases of German research at the Kaiser Wilhelm Institutes -- surely as part of the vetting process for those grants, there must have been full discussion of the nature of the programs. Flexner was a sophisticated man who could not have been ignorant of the moral implications of such work. Is it plausible that in his discussions with zealous eugenicists like Heinrich Poll, Robert Yerkes, Henry Pritchett, Alexis Carrel and Charles Lindbergh, this man whom Bonner described as enjoying "intellectual jousting," voiced no contrary opinion?

In a speech to benefactors of Montefiore Hospital in 1932, Flexner remarked that although the world "was not yet civilized," he remained optimistic: "We find ourselves in the clutches of social, economic and financial difficulties...[but] when in a storm, wise navigators don't jump into the sea, [they] adapt to the crisis. The storm will pass and be followed by clear, calm weather."[4]

Urging his listeners to stay the course, he predicted that within a decade "no doubt we will be stronger and wiser than in 1929 when we were living in a fool's paradise." The way forward was through rationalism, education and enlightened philanthropy, "worthwhile life and civilization depend on them." Declaring that it was a time for defiance, he recalled how when the army of Marshall Foch was shattered during World War I, Foch telegraphed to his commander-in-chief, "My army is destroyed. I shall attack." Such rhetoric must have been inspiring.

In 1938 Abraham Flexner addressed the National Conference of Christians and Jews and asked, "What has this dreadful and unprecedented experience to teach us as Americans?" His answer: "tolerance, tolerance, tolerance, a thousand times over...The German terror should determine us not only to live but to let live."[5] Once more, those were inspiring words but a more appropriate lesson to be drawn at that particular time in history might have been diligence, diligence, diligence – not only against Nazism but against perversion of American policy based on eugenics ideology and against institutional anti-Semitism.

What would I have wanted Abraham Flexner to have said or done? He should have taken to task the likes of Dean Winternitz of Yale or President Harold Dodds of Princeton about their quota systems, rather than ignoring or denying their existence.

He could have forcefully disputed eugenicists such as Alexis Carrel and Harry Laughlin who were promoting coerced sterilization and euthanasia as well as restrictive immigration policies. He should have fought to withhold Rockefeller support for race-based eugenics research that was being coordinated in Germany by his friend Heinrich Poll. Moreover, he might have supported his brother Bernard Flexner as well as Bernard Baruch, Albert Einstein, Rabbi Stephen Wise and others who publicly advocated for the Jews of Europe. These would have been far more effective than a meek call for tolerance, especially from a leader of his stature and influence.

Another aspect of Abraham Flexner's educational philosophy which has drawn scholarly attention in recent years was that he frequently wrote or lectured about the importance of "humanism." As a result some contemporary bioethicists regard him as a kindred spirit. Dr. Edmund Pellegrino who views the Flexner Report as persuasive but frequently "misunderstood" has suggested that its author anticipated and dealt with every matter of importance in the education of a physician, including the importance of cultural and philosophic grounding. Pellegrino acknowledged that Flexner could have been more explicit, but argues that the Report's emphasis on a strong scientific foundation for medicine was not intended to be at the expense of the physician's humanity or humanism: "Flexner championed the ideal of the physician as an educated person – one in whom science and humanity were necessarily and indissolubly united."[6] Professor Kenneth Ludmerer is another who asserts that Flexner was misunderstood and incorrectly accused (among others by the likes of Osler and Peabody) of ignoring the doctor-patient relationship.[7]

But it's easy to read more into Flexner's words then he might have intended, or to project one's own beliefs onto his. A case in point is a recent comprehensive review by Australian bioethicists Thomas Faunce and Paul Gatenby titled *Flexner's ethical oversight reprised? Contemporary medical education and the health impacts of corporate globalization.*[8]

The authors conceded that Flexner's commitment to medical ethics as a basis of medical professionalism was "generally underemphasized", but in their attempt to connect current medical ethical thinking with Flexner's ideas of a century ago, they repeatedly employed qualifying words: "Less attention... has been paid to *apparent omissions* from Flexner's reports, in particular their limited consideration of the strain between medical ethics and health law as a basis of professionalism." (italics are my own); Flexner personally *appeared* to embrace a form of virtue ethics in his educational methods"; "although *probably present implicitly*, particularly in his criticism of commercialism, medical ethics as a topic was not routinely or directly mentioned in Flexner's recommendations."; his core recommendations *"might be interpreted as involving implicit ethical implications;"* "The important dilemmas facing medical ethics and professionalism in Flexner's time *probably required much more direct and detailed recommendations."*

Of course Abraham Flexner was not a physician (although he did receive honorary medical degrees from Berlin in 1930 and Brussels in 1931) and when he discussed "humanism," it was from an abstract perspective. In his Taylorian lecture at Oxford in 1930 ("The Burden of Humanism") he made an effort to view science and humanism as complementary activities which form a circle, "in which the lifeblood of humanity flows and intermingles." As Flexner saw it the world of his time was dominated by industry and science which had largely "destroyed the puny notions within which religion, philosophy and history once led a relatively easy intellectual existence.... the world will become a chaos if men do not strive to understand both themselves and one another.

This being said, and said well, Flexner never addressed the doctor-patient relationship in a clinical sense; neither the physician paternalism which characterized his era which he surely would have approved, nor today's dominant paradigm of patient self-determination. His advocacy of "humanism" notwithstanding, Abraham Flexner was an intellectual elitist and the notion of him being a proto-bioethicist remains unconvincing to me – at least in the current application of that term. To be sure, an educational grounding in the humanities can provide insight and context, but not necessarily the empathy and compassion which characterize a sensitive physician.

If Abraham Flexner were alive today, what would he be attacking? Surely, he would rail against the politicization of public education and he would be appalled at commercialism in medicine. He would insist on evidence-based decision making and probably his pleas for integrating the humanities and medical science would resonate with many. He also would be outspoken about the current dearth of primary care physicians, especially to underserved populations.

After reading this book, some surely will protest that I have gone too far in my criticism – that the worst that can be said about Abraham Flexner, the man, is that he put too much faith in Enlightenment values, or that he did not rise above the prejudice of his times -- and if sometimes his behavior was problematic, at least we should be able to forgive him his human weaknesses. Perhaps a case also might be made that the fact he didn't suffer fools lightly was an admirable trait. Both at the GEB and the IAS his *modus operandi* was to use his personal connections to work behind the scenes and, in the same way, he claimed to have worked privately to assist Jewish colleagues who were in need; regarding this, we must take him at his word.

So after all, do we have any right to criticize "A.F."? I propose a qualified yes – not necessarily about what he stood for or did, as much as what he didn't publicly stand against. To be sure, the very different social and political dynamics operative in this country early in the last century have to be considered, but it does not follow that we are obliged to *condone* the choices that were made by people like Flexner who often chose to play it safe.

The political theorist Hannah Arendt famously wrote about the "banality" of evil, how through acquiescence, ordinary individuals can start down a slippery slope toward accepting immoral behavior as normative. Abraham Flexner was *not* an evil man and he committed no crime – nor did those of his contemporaries who complacently accepted the premises of their time when eugenics theory appeared to be supported by scientific evidence and when anti-Semitism was taken for granted. Preaching tolerance was commendable and his wish to socially fit-in understandable, but sophisticated intellectuals like Abraham Flexner could have and should have been far more astute about the destructive nature of events which were occurring, not only in Germany, but in their own country.

In the Preface of this book I described Abraham Flexner as being "exasperating." Perhaps a more suitable adjective might have been "disappointing." I am disappointed that this brilliant scholar, this exponent of progressive ideas, this self-styled gadfly, backed off from confronting some of the great issues of his time. Flexner liked to portray himself as a pragmatist who only expended his energy on projects which were achievable -- to me this seems too facile a justification for passivity. It certainly does not measure up to his grand words on the opening of the Institute for Advanced Study, "I have deliberately hitched the Institute to the stars." No, his timidity in speaking out about certain politically or socially incorrect issues appears to have reflected a fundamental character flaw which once was described by the man who knew him best, his brother Simon:

> [He is] a strong person, very generous, intensely egotistical, with a great capacity for self-deception. My belief is that he readily translates events into harmony with his own point of view and his own cogitations. He hardly ever admits mistakes or failure on his own part, although finding many faults in others.[9]

In the end, we should do more than merely attempt to understand our predecessors. While it may be unwise to judge them by our own standards, at least we are obliged to judge *ourselves* -- for failing to do this, we lose an opportunity to learn from history. The crucial question, then, is not how to account for Abraham Flexner's frailties – rather, it is whether challenged by the same circumstances and without the benefit of hindsight, we would have done any better?

Nothing has aided the persistence of falsehood, and the evils resulting from it, more than the unwillingness of good people to admit the truth when it was disturbing to their comfortable assurance.

B.H. Liddell Hart (1944)

SOURCES

The definitive biography of Abraham Flexner is Thomas Neville Bonner's *Iconoclast, Abraham Flexner and a Life in Learning* which was published in 2002. It provides numerous primary citations from which I have drawn extensively, Notes being referenced as "Bonner" or "Quoted by Bonner." Similarly for other authors, after first use, subsequent citations begin with a surname, or by surname followed by an abbreviated book title.

Primary materials concerning Flexner's time at the Rockefeller Foundation were found at the Rockefeller Archive Center, Sleepy Hollow, NY, particulalry in the files of the General Education Board. I am grateful for the Center's permission to reproduce portions of these and thankful to project archivist Nancy Adgent for her assistance.

Concerning Flexner's years at the Institute for Advanced Study, Princeton, NJ, (henceforth abbreviated IAS), The Shelby White and Leon Levy Archives Center was a rich source of material and I appreciate their permission to publish selections of correspondence from files of faculty and trustees. In the following Notes, these will be abbreviated as from IAS Archives. Special thanks to Archival Assistant Erica Mosner who was of great help.

The cover photo of Abraham Flexner was taken by me of a bust at the IAS which was made by the famous Russian sculptor Sergei Konenkov, c. 1935. To my mind it provides an appropriately sphinx-like image of this sometimes inscrutable man.

NOTES

Preface

1. Abraham Flexner, *I Remember. The Autobiography of Abraham Flexner* (New York: Simon and Schuster, 1940). (hereafter cited as AF, *I Remember*).

2. John F. Kennedy, *Why England Slept* (New York: Wilfred Funk. Inc. 1940).

3. B.H.Liddell Hart, *Why Don't We Learn From History?* (London: Allan & Unwin,1944).

Chapter 1. Enigma

1. *New York Times,* September 22, 1959.

2. Thomas Neville Bonner, *Iconoclast. Abraham Flexner and a Life in Learning* (Baltimore: The Johns Hopkins University Press, 2002), xx. (hereafter, all references to this book will be in abbreviated form cited as "Bonner"). 308.

3. Allan Nevins, introduction to *Abraham Flexner, An Autobiography, A complete revision, brought up to date, of the author's* I Remember, *published in 1940. (New York:*

Simon and Schuster, 1960) (hereafter referred to as AF, Updated) xiii.

4. Daniel M Fox. "Abraham Flexner's Unpublished Report. Foundations and Medical Education, 1909-1928." *Bull of the History of Medicine* Vol. 54, No. 4, 480, 1980.

5. Quoted in Bonner, 307

6. James Thomas Flexner, *An American Saga. The Story of Helen Thomas & Simon Flexner* (Boston: Little, Brown and Comp. 1984) 120. (hereafter cited as JTF, *American Saga*)

7. JTF, *American Saga*, 257-8.

8. JTF, *American Saga*, 121.

9. AF, Updated, 1.

10. *New York Times*, 6 October 1940, 4.

11. Quoted in Bonner, 11.

Chapter 2. Louisville

1. Bonner, 1-19.

2. Charles A. Madison, *Eminent American Jews, 1776 to the Present* (New York: Frederick Ungar Publishing Co., 1970) 209-224.

3. John M. Barry, *The Great Influenza* (London: Penguin Books, 2005) 75.

4. JTF, *American Saga* 377.

5. Abraham Flexner, *The American College: A Criticism* (New York: Century, 1908).

6. AF, *I Remember*, 66.

Chapter 3: The Report

1. Berliner, Howard. *A System of Scientific Medicine: Philanthropic Foundations in the Flexner Era* (Tavistock Publishers, 1985) 105. (hereafter cited as Berliner.)

2. Henry S. Pritchett, Introduction to Abraham Flexner, *Medical Education in the United States and Canada (New York: Carnegie Foundation for the Advancement of Teaching,* 1910) xi.

3. Barry, 84.

4. Paul Starr, *The Social Transformation of American Medicine.* (New York: Basic Books, 1982) 118-127.

5. Berliner,109.

6. Ibid., 121.

7. Lester S. King. "The Flexner Report of 1910", *Journal of the American Medical Association,* Vol. 251, No. 8, 1079-1086, Feb. 24, 1984.

8. Howard Merkel, "Abraham Flexner and his Remarkable Report on Medical Education. A Century Later." *Journal American Medical Association,* Vol. 303, No. 9, 888-690. March 3, 2010.

9. Berliner, 114.

10. Quoted in Bonner, 206.

11. Berliner, 152.

12. Kenneth M. Ludmerer, "Understanding the Flexner Report," *Academic Medicine*, Vol. 85, No. 2, 193, 2010.

13. Ibid.,196.

14. AF, Updated 108

Chapter 4. The Board

1. Abraham Flexner, *Prostitution in Europe*. (New York: The Cottery Co., 1914).

2. Nicholas Scott. "John D. Rockefeller, Jr. & Eugenics: A Means of Social Manipulation," p. 18 http://studentorgs.umf. maine.edu/aio/public:www.historian/vol2iss2/rockefeller_ article.pdf (checked 7/20/10)

3. AF, Updated 53.

4. Quoted in Samuel Chotzinoff, "Robin Hood, 1930," *The New Yorker,* November 22, 1930, p. 29, folder 2770, box 268. Rockefeller Foundation Archives, Rockefeller Archive Center, Sleepy Hollow, NY (hereafter designated RAC).

5. AF to Harvey Cushing, April 8, 1921. folder 7295, box 711, series 1, General Education Board Archives, RAC.

6. Fox, 487.

7. Quoted in Bonner, 87

8. Starr, 121.

9. AF, *I Remember,* 237

10. Steven C. Wheatley, *The Politics of Philanthropy. Abraham Flexner and Medical Education* (Madison: The University of Wisconsin Press, 1988) 122.

11. Quoted in Bonner, 172.

12. Fox, 493

13. Quoted in Bonner, 207

14. AF to Wallace Buttrick, August 3, 1925, folder 2768, box 268, series 1, General Education Board Archives, RAC.

15. Fox, 492

16. Wheatley, 162.

17. Ibid., 164.

18. AF, Updated, 223.

19. Quoted in Bonner, 211

20. JTF, *American Saga*, 382.

21. Quoted in Bonner, 292

22. AF to Raymond Fosdick, (undated), folder 2768, box 268, series 1.2. Graduate Education Board Archives, RAC.

Chapt. 5 Eugenics

1. For additional readings on eugenics, see Michael Nevins, *A Tale of Two "Villages": Vineland and Skillman, NJ.* (Bloomington: iUniverse, 2009.); Stefan Kuhl, *The Nazi Connection. Eugenics, American Racism and German National Socialism* (New York, Oxford: Oxford University

Press 1994); Edwin Black, *War Against the Weak. Eugenics and America's Campaign to Create a Master Race* (New York: Four Walls Eight Windows, 2003); Harry Bruinius. *Better For All The World. The Secret History of Forced Sterilization and America's Quest for Racial Purity.* (New York: Alfred A. Knopf, 2006).

2. Jeremy H. Baron, *The Anglo-American Biomedical Antecedents of Nazi Crimes. An Historical Analysis of Racism, Nationalism, Eugenics and Genocide* (The Edwin Mellen Press, 2007.) 64.

3. Nevins, 36.

4. Ibid., 37.

5. Stephen Jay Gould, *The Mismeasurement of Man* (New York: W.W. Norton & Comp., 1981) 222.

6. *Popular Science Monthly*, Vol. 81, p. 102, 1912 (New York Academy of Medicine Archives.)

7. Quoted in Bonner, 224

8. AF to Wallace Buttrick, July 9, 1922, folder 2768, box 268, series 1, Graduate Education Board Archives, RAC.

9. Paul Weindling, *Health, Race and German Politics between national unification and Nazism.* (Cambridge University Press, 1989.) 325.

10. Black, 284

11. Kerstein J. Bien, " 'Monkeys, Babies, Idiots' and 'Primitives.' Nature-Nurture Debates and Philanthropic Funding Support for Anthropology in the 1920s and 1930s." *Journal of the*

History pf Behavioral Sciences, Vol. 45 (3), 219-235, 2009.

12. Ernst Rudin to Lawrence Dunham, November 22,. 1932. Bureau of Social Hygiene, Eugenics folder 178, box 8, series 3, Bureau of Social Hygiene Records, RAC.

13. *JTF, American Saga* 442

14. *Eugenical News, The International Federation of Eugenical Organizations.* Vol. 15, (1), 39, 1930. N.Y.Academy of Medicine Archives.

15. Nevins, 49.

16. Quoted in Bonner, 294.

17. Wheatley, 114.

18. AF, *I Remember*, 106.

19. Bonner, 195.

20. Gould, 252.

Chapter 6. The Institute

1. Bonner, 220.

2. Ibid., 221.

3. AF, Updated 234.

4. Quoted in *Institute for Advanced Study: An Introduction.* Institute for Advanced Study Text, 2005.

5. Walter Isaacson, *Einstein. His Life and Universe* (New York: Simon & Schuster, 2007) 426.

6. Kati Morton, *The Great Escape* (New York: Simon & Schuster, 2006) 92.

7. Jean Medawar & David Pyke, *Hitler's Gift* (London: Richard Cohen Books, 2000) 115.

8. 8. Isaacson, 416

9. 9.Paul S. Riebenfeld, "Signing Up Einstein," *New York Times*, (Letter to Editor), November 1, 1987.

10. Flexner to H.Maass, IAS Archives, Trustees Files/Maass Box 8, July 24, 1933.

11. 11. Flexner to Elsa Einstein, Nov. 14, 1993; Albert Einstein Archives, Hebrew University, Jerusalem. 38-055.

12. 12. Quoted in Bonner, 254.

13. 13. Ibid., 253

14. Flexner to H.Maass, IAS Archives, Trustees Files/Maass Box 8, Nov. 14, 1933.

15. Flexner to H.Maass, IAS Archives, Trustees Files/Maass, Box 8, Dec. 4, 1933.

16. Quoted in Bonner, 253.

17. Ibid., 255

18. Isaacson, 416.

19. Ibid., 445.

Chapter 7 End Game

1. AF to Felix Frankfurter, IAS Archives, Trustees Files, Box 3. May 7, 1934.

2. Quoted in Bonner, 241.

3. Steve Batterson, *Pursuit of Genius. Flexner, Einstein, and the Early Faculty at the Institute for Advanced Study.* ((Wellesley: A.K.Peters Ltd., 2006) 183.

4. Ibid., 216.

5. AF, *I Remember,* 370.

6. Batterson, 226.

7. Ibid., 230.

8. E.M.Earle to AF, IAS Archives, Faculty Files, Box 6, Earle/ June 9, 1939.

9. E.M.Earle to Frank Aydelotte, IAS Archives, Faculty Files, Box 6. Earle/June 28, 1939.

10. E.M.Earle to Oswald Veblen, IAS Archives, Faculty Files, Box 6. Earle/July 13, 1939.

11. E.M.Earle to Herbert Maass, IAS Archives, Faculty Files, Box 6. Earle/July 26, 1939.

12. Flexner to E.M.Earle, IAS Archives, Faculty Files, Box 6. Earle/October 19, 1939.

13. E.M.Earle to David Mittrany, IAS Archives, Faculty Files, Box 6. Earle/October 19, 1939.

14. D.Mittrany to E.M.Earle, IAS Archives, Faculty Files, Box 6. Mittrany/July 24, 1939.

15. Quoted in Bonner, 286.

16. Steve Batterson, "The Vision, Insight, and Influence of Oswald Veblen." *Notices of the American Mathematical Society*, Vol. 54, no. 5, 2007: 606-617.

17. Deane Montgomery, "Oswald Veblen," *Bulletin American Mathematical Society*, January, 1962 118-121.

18. AF, *I Remember*, 356.

19. Herbert H. Maas, "The Founding and Early History of the Institute," 1955 IAS, in bound volume "Memories of Herbert H.Maas."

20. AF, *I Remember,* 397.

21. *New York Times*, September 27, 1987.

Chapter 8. Flexner's Jewish Identity Problem

1. AF, *I Remember*, 13.

2. JTF, *American Saga*, 46.

3. AF, *I Remember*, 401.

4. Quoted in Bonner, 140.

5. Abraham Flexner to Samuel Dorfman, 3 January 1944. Reproduced in Ph.D diss.of Ronald F. Movrich, "Before the Gates of Excellence: Abraham Flexner and Education, 1866-1918," (Berkeley: University of California, Berkeley, 1981), Rockefeller Archive Center, RAC.

6. E.M. Earle memorandum to Maass and Leidesdorf, IAS Archives, Faculty Files, Box 6. Earle/July 2, 1939.

7. 7. Quoted in Bonner, 140.

8. 8. Fox, 483

9. 9. Bonner, 224.

10. Howard Spiro and Priscilla W. Norton. "Dean Milton C. Winternitz at Yale," *Perspectives in Biology and Medicine*, volume 46, number 3 (summer 2003) 407.

11. Bonner,150.

12. Dan Oren, *Joining the Club: A History of Jews and Yale* (New Haven: Yale University Press, 1985) 139-155.

13. Spiro, 410.

14. Quoted in Bonner, 11.

15. Edward C. Halperin, "The Jewish Problem in U.S. Medical Education," *J Hist Med Allied Sci* 2001 April: 56 (2):152.

16. Ibid., 157.

17. Ibid., 164.

18. Bonner, 179.

19. Melvin Urofsky. *Louis D. Brandeis. A Life.* (New York: Pantheon Books, 2009.) 730-740.

20. Bonner, 11

Chapter 9 The Last Decades

1. Bonner, 289

2. Ibid., 294

3. AF, Updated , 288-289.

4. Robert D. Calkins (memo) March 23, 1950, folder 2769, box 268, series 1, General Education Board Archives, RAC.

5. Abraham Flexner, Esther S. Bailey. *Funds and foundations, their policies, past and present* (Harpers Brothers, 1912) 63.

6. Lewis L. Strauss, "Lasting Ideals of Abraham Flexner," *Journal of the American Medical Association*, Vol.173, No. 13, 1414, July 30, 1960.

7. Quoted in Bonner, 299.

8. Ibid., 303.

9. Ibid., 305.

10. Ibid., 306.

11. AF, Updated, xiii.

12. Ibid., 291.

13. Ibid, 289.

14. AF, *I Remember*, 404.

Chapter 10 Judging Flexner/Judging a Generation

1. Quoted in Bonner, 307.

2. Fox, 498.

3. Stephen Wheatley, *The Politics of Philanthropy. Abraham Flexner and Medical Education,* (Madison: The University of Wisconsin Press, 1988) 138-139.

4. Abraham Flexner, "The Significance, Present and Future of Montefiore Hospital," speech 10 April, 1932, New York Academy of Medicine, file 115903, box 361.

5. Bonner, 266.

6. Edmund D. Pellegrino, "The Reconciliation of Technology and Humanism: A Flexnerian Task 75 Years Later," In *Flexner: 75 Years Later,* Charles Vevier (ed), (University Press of America, Inc.. 1987. 77-106.

7. Kenneth M. Ludmerer, "Understanding the Flexner Report," *Academic Medicine,* Vol. 85. No.2/February, 193-196, 2010.

8. Thomas A. Faunce and Paul Gatenby, "Flexner's ethical oversight reprised? Contemporary medical education and the health impacts of corporate globalization." *Medical Education* 2005: 39: 1066-1074.

9. JTF, *American Saga* 120

CPSIA information can be obtained
at www.ICGtesting.com
Printed in the USA
BVHW040258260522
638098BV00002B/407